Better Homes and Gardens®

NEW
PATCHWORK
& QUILTING
BOOK

© Copyright 1987 by Meredith Corporation, Des Moines, Iowa.
All Rights Reserved. Printed in the United States of America.
First Edition. Fifth Printing, 1991.
Library of Congress Catalog Card Number: 86-62170
ISBN: 0-696-01615-X (hard cover)
ISBN: 0-696-01616-8 (trade paperback)

Cover project: See pages 40–41.

CONTENTS

PATCHWORK TREASURES

TO ENJOY EVERY DAY

Much of the fun of patchwork is in turning commonplace items into colorful and stylish accessories to use and enjoy. Everyday objects become special when you use patchwork to play up an inspired color combination, highlight a spectacular fabric, pattern, or technique—or even apply patchwork patterns to other crafts. This chapter includes ideas for projects to make and use all around the house.

Start off each morning in grand style with the table runner and place mats, *left*. They're based on the favorite Schoolhouse pattern. It's always a fascinating pattern to piece, because of the variety and combination of shapes used to create the motif. The pattern includes rectangles and squares, as well as trapezoids for the roof and a pentagon above the front window.

Although these accessories are pieced and assembled in a traditional manner, bold lines of machine quilting add a contemporary touch. Notice how using diagonal lines for the place mats and horizontal quilting on the table runner keep the design lively.

Instructions for these and all of the projects in this chapter begin on page 16.

PATCHWORK TREASURES

Every play day should begin with something special, like the appliquéd apron, *opposite*. This is an ideal project for learning machine appliqué, because the motif is stitched to the pocket front, not the apron piece. Use scraps of contrasting fabric for binding and ties.

Stitched-on details spark up the trio of totes, *above,* and give them personalities all their own. The elephant tote features purchased metallic star shapes, and all of the three use small touches of hand embroidery for the facial expressions and tiny buttons for eyes.

Besides using these full-size patterns for the items shown, try stitching them onto accessories for a child's room, such as a pillow top, curtain panels, or pajama bag.

PATCHWORK TREASURES

Few patchwork patterns are as familiar and well-loved as the Dresden Plate design, used for two of the projects, *opposite.* These home accessories make good use of this circular design, and are easy ways to learn to piece and appliqué this pattern.

Five small Dresden Plates decorate the Shaker peg rack. They are appliquéd to a muslin background, quilted, and stretched over a pine board. Mount Shaker pegs in the center of each motif.

Save your prettiest leftover fabrics for the Dresden Plate album cover. To personalize the album, cross-stitch your family name and date on a piece of even-weave fabric and use it for the center circle. Or, use a fabric scrap for the center and embroider the name and date with colorful outline stitches.

With the amiable teddy bear, *opposite,* in your sewing corner, you'll never waste time hunting a thimble, straight pins, or tape measure. Friend to all patchworkers, this bear is stitched from scraps of fabric, and dressed up with snippets of ribbons and lace. Her skirt serves as a sewing caddy, designed to hold essentials for all types of projects. Any of the patchworkers and quilters on your gift list would love to have her own "caddy-bear."

Count on the exciting patchwork tablecloth, *right,* to liven up an afternoon snack. The center of the cloth features a jumbo Pinwheel block, with bands and borders in coordinating colors. Because the scale of this pattern is enlarged, piecing goes quickly. The 47x69-inch cloth is lined to stabilize stitching and to conceal raw edges.

You can use the same piecing instructions to create an easy lap quilt. Just piece the top of the quilt as directed for the tablecloth. Then add batting and a backing as directed for any of the other quilts in this book. Quilt by hand or by machine.

Use the central Pinwheel pattern, slightly reduced, to make the napkins, *below.* They're good ways to use up fabric scraps, and look great all by themselves. Ours are lined and trimmed with topstitching.

PATCHWORK TREASURES

Luscious shades of fabric always enhance a patchwork pattern. The wall hanging, *above,* is a prime example. It's stitched in the Rocky Glen pattern, a traditional design that can take on a contemporary look when made in colors like these. Even the borders and sashing strips of this 32x35-inch wall hanging are special—strips of various shades of pale tan and off-white fabric are pieced together to form color variations.

Whenever small squares are stitched in rows around a center block, it's a version of the Sunshine and Shadows pattern. The center of the piano bench cover, *above*, is just such a variation. Four of the squares are accented with a bright triangle to add playful color interest.

Piece the remaining area of the bench cover with strips in matching colors; adjust the length to fit the piano bench you have.

PATCHWORK TREASURES

Although piecing the Streak of Lightning pattern used for these projects appears difficult, it's greatly simplified because the diagonal lines are broken into squares. Each square is composed of two different-colored triangles that are pieced together. Then the squares are arranged to form rows of zigzags.

The deep tones found in front of an evening fire inspired the color scheme for the pillows, *above,* and the throw, *opposite.*

The size of the pillows is dictated only by the size of the pieced square used to make each of the Streak of Lightning blocks. For maximum comfort, make a group of them in various sizes.

The 36x59-inch throw is a lap-size quilt and is large enough to show off this pattern with the most impact. All projects made with this pattern are machine-quilted in zigzag lines, which helps to conceal the square block seams.

PATCHWORK TREASURES

House Runner And Place Mats

Shown on pages 4–5.

Finished size of the place mat is 14x15 inches. Runner is 15x36½ inches.

MATERIALS
For one place mat
½ yard of red cotton fabric
¼ yard of yellow cotton fabric
⅛ yard of blue cotton fabric
15x16-inch piece of fleece
Water-erasable pen
Graph paper

For the runner
⅞ yard of red cotton fabric
⅜ yard of yellow cotton fabric
¼ yard of blue cotton fabric
16x37½-inch piece of fleece
Water-erasable pen

INSTRUCTIONS
Enlarge the house block, following diagram, *below,* onto the graph paper. Trace around the pattern shapes; add ¼-inch seam allowances to all patterns; cut out. Make cardboard templates for all the pattern pieces.

Note: Cutting directions for the strips that frame the blocks and the bias trim include ¼-inch seam allowances. All sewing is with right sides facing.

To piece one house block
The finished block is 9½x10½ inches. From blue fabric, cut one *each* of D, F, and G; cut two *each* of B, E, and H; cut three of A.

From yellow fabric, cut three of C; cut two of J; cut one *each* of I, K, L, and M.

Piece block, referring to the diagram, *below.*

To make the place mat
Piece one house block as directed, *above.* From the yellow fabric, cut two 1½x10-inch strips and two 1½x13-inch strips.

From the red fabric, cut one 15x16-inch backing piece, two 1½x12-inch strips, and two 1½x15-inch strips for borders.

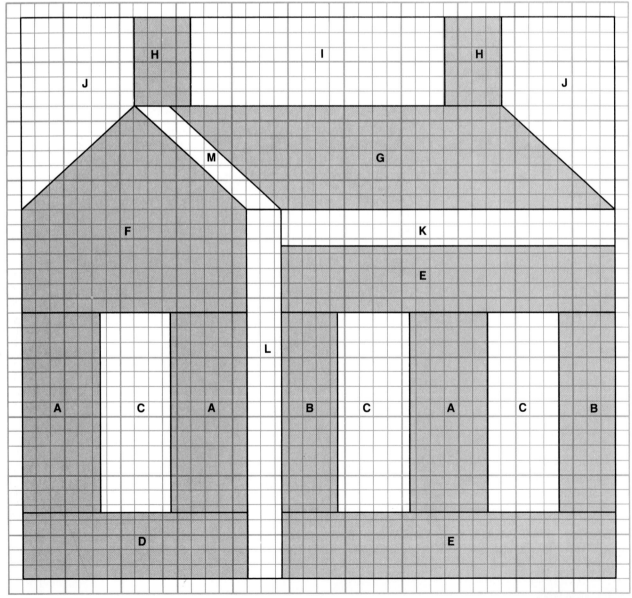

HOUSE BLOCK

1 Square = ¼ Inch

Sew the short yellow strips to the sides of the block, then sew the long yellow strips to the top and bottom of the block. Sew the red strips to the yellow strips, repeating the same sequence.

For the quilt markings, draw a diagonal line (from corner to corner) atop the block, using the water-erasable pen. Then draw two parallel lines 2 inches from each side of the center line. Repeat the 2-inch markings across the top.

Layer the top, fleece, and backing; baste together. Machine-quilt with contrasting thread through all layers atop the drawn lines.

Trim away the excess backing and fleece; round off the corners. Cut 1½-inch-wide red bias strips and piece together to make a 60-inch length. Sew bias to back side of mat. Fold bias to front side, turn under seam allowance, and topstitch in place.

To make the runner

Piece two house blocks as directed on page 16.

From the red fabric, cut one 16x37½-inch piece for backing; cut two 1½x36½-inch strips and four 1½x13-inch strips.

From the yellow fabric, cut one 9½x13-inch rectangle for center unit; cut four 1½x10-inch strips and four 1½x13-inch strips.

Sew two short yellow strips to the sides of *each* house block; then sew two long yellow strips to the top and bottom of *each* block.

Sew two short red strips to the top and bottom of *each* block.

Sew the yellow rectangle to top of one house block, then sew opposite side of rectangle to the top of the second house block. Sew long red strips to each side edge to complete top assembly.

To mark for quilting, draw a line, *widthwise,* through the center of the yellow rectangle with a water-erasable pen. Draw lines parallel to this line every 2 inches. Draw one quilting line through the middle of each of the two center red strips.

Layer the top, fleece, and backing; baste together. Machine-quilt with contrasting thread atop the drawn lines. Trim excess fleece and backing.

From the red fabric, cut bias strips 1½ inches wide and piece together to make a strip measuring 103 inches. Sew bias to back side of runner. Fold bias to front side, turn under seam allowance, and topstitch in place.

Child's Appliqué Apron and Tote

Shown on page 6–7.

Finished apron is 19 inches long. The tote measures 9x10 inches.

MATERIALS
For one apron and tote set
¾ yard of striped or plaid cotton fabric for the apron
½ yard of complementary-colored cotton fabric for the tote
Scraps of coordinating cotton fabrics for appliqués
4 yards of ½-inch-wide double-fold bias tape
½ yard of fusible webbing
1 yard of cotton cording for piping
Embroidery floss in colors of your choice
¼-inch-diameter buttons for eyes
Six 1-inch star appliqués for elephant trim
Graph paper

INSTRUCTIONS
For the apron
Enlarge the apron and pocket patterns, *right,* onto graph paper; cut out. Cut out apron; set aside. Trace pocket onto remaining fabric piece, adding ⅝-inch seam allowances (do not cut out).

Select one full-size animal design on pages 18–20. Trace and transfer the patterns to the appliqué fabrics as follows: Cut the main body from the tote fabric; cut additional shapes from scrap fabrics. Cut matching pieces from fusible webbing.

Center the appliqué pieces atop the pocket; fuse in place. Machine-satin-stitch the animal outlines, using contrasting threads.

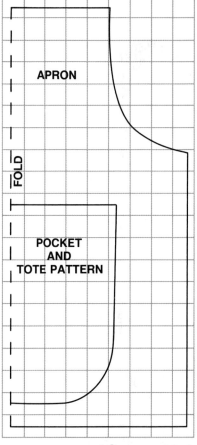

APRON AND TOTE

APRON

FOLD

POCKET AND TOTE PATTERN

1 Square = 1 Inch

For the seal: Use three strands of embroidery floss in colors of your choice to outline-stitch the whiskers and the ball lines. Satin-stitch the nose. Make French-knots on the whisker dots. Sew on button for eye.

For the lion: Outline-stitch the nose, mouth, and tail. Fill in nose with satin-stitches. Sew on two buttons for eyes. Add eyelashes and tail tuft with long stitches.

For the elephant: Sew star appliqués in place. Outline-stitch the star trails and use long stitches for the eyelashes. Braid three 6-strands of embroidery floss to measure 3 inches for the tail; tie a knot at end. Cut off floss ends, leaving a ¾-inch tassel. Sew the tail in place. Sew on button eye.

When all appliquéing and embroidery is complete, cut out the pocket. Along top edge of pocket, press under ¼ inch, then an additional ⅜ inch to the wrong side; *continued* stitch in place. Press under remaining sides. Center the pocket atop the apron; pin, then topstitch in place.

With bias tape, encase *top* and *bottom* apron edges; top-stitch in place. Encase the *straight side* edges; top-stitch in place.

Cut two 36½-inch-long pieces of bias tape. Encase *each* curved apron edge with bias tape, leaving about 12 inches extending at the top edges and 16 inches at the side edges for ties. Turn under ¼ inch at both ends of *each* bias tape; sew from one end of the tape to the other end to finish.

For the tote

For the handles, cut two strips, *each* 2½x16 inches, from the tote fabric; set aside.

Use the apron pocket pattern to make the bag. Trace a front and back onto the fabric, adding ⅝-inch seam allowances. Cut out one for back; do not cut out front.

Select one of the full-size animal patterns on pages 18–20. Refer to apron instructions on page 17 to appliqué the tote front.

Note: Cut the main body piece from the apron fabric.

When appliquéing is complete, cut out the tote front.

To make the handles, press under ¼ inch on both the long edges of *each* strip. Press *each* handle strip in half, *lengthwise,* wrong sides facing, and topstitch the folded edges together.

With right sides facing, place raw edges of handle ends atop the front tote top edge, 1 inch in from the side seam lines. Stitch the handle ends to the tote, using ½-inch seams. Press raw edge of top and handle under ¼ inch to wrong side, then under an additional ⅜ inch. Turn handle up and sew across the top edge.

Repeat these instructions to attach the handle to the tote back.

Cut 1½-inch-wide bias strips from the remaining tote fabric; piece to make a 36-inch strip.

Cover the cotton cording with the bias strip to make the piping. With right sides facing, sew piping to tote front along seam line.

With right sides facing, sew tote front to back. Clip curves; overcast-stitch raw seam edges; turn.

Dresden Plate Photograph Album

Shown on page 8.

The finished photograph album is 10¾x11½ inches.

MATERIALS
¾ yard of blue cotton fabric
½ yard of red cotton fabric for lining
Scraps of 8 assorted cotton fabrics
8-inch square of 18-count even-weave fabric
3 yards of purchased red piping
½ yard of polyester fleece
Embroidery floss
Water-erasable pen
Purchased photograph album, approximately 10¾x11½ inches

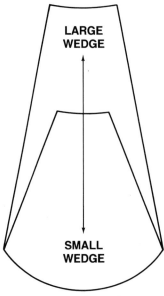

LARGE WEDGE

SMALL WEDGE

DRESDEN PLATE PATTERNS

INSTRUCTIONS
Note: The instructions are written to custom-cover any album of similar size.

To piece the Dresden Plate
From cardboard, make a template for the large Dresden Plate wedge, *left.*

Draw two wedges on *each* of the eight fabric scraps. Cut out the wedges, adding ¼-inch seam allowances.

Piece wedges to form a ring, placing matching fabric wedges opposite each other. Sew wedges together atop the marked seam lines, leaving the ¼-inch seam allowances unsewn at each end. Press seams to one side.

Turn under the seam allowances on the inner circle and around the outside edges; baste.

To make the album cover

With a water-erasable pen, center and trace the center circle of the Dresden Plate onto the cross-stitch fabric. Work cross-stitch letters or another design of your choice within the drawn circle.

To make the album cover patterns, draw two rectangles onto brown paper. Draw one the size of the album front cover, and the second the size of the spine. Add ½-inch seam allowances to patterns. For the inner flaps, draw a pattern as long as the front cover pattern but 8 inches wide.

From the blue fabric, cut two large rectangles for the front and back covers; cut one spine and two flaps. Cut matching shapes from fleece.

Center the Dresden Plate atop the cross-stitched circle; baste in place just beyond the center circle. Applique the center circle to the cross-stitched piece. Cut away the excess cross-stitched fabric on the wrong side to within ¼ inch of the stitching line.

Center and pin the Dresden Plate to the album front; appliqué in place.

Baste fleece pieces to wrong sides of the corresponding album fabric pieces.

Quilt around *each* wedge ¼ inch from the wedge seam lines.

FINISHING: Sew piping to *each* long edge of spine piece. With right sides together, sew album front and back covers to spine. Trim seams to ¼ inch. Sew the piping atop the seam line around all sides, right sides facing. Trim seam allowance to ¼ inch.

From the red fabric, cut lining to match the assembled cover.

On one long side of *each* inner flap piece, press under ½ inch twice; machine-hem. With right sides together, and raw edges even, sew flaps to ends of cover.

Pin right side of lining atop wrong sides of flaps. Sew lining, through all thicknesses, atop the piping seam; leave opening for turning. Clip corners, turn, and press; sew opening closed. Slip flaps over album.

Dresden Plate Shaker Peg Rack

Shown on page 8.

The finished peg rack is approximately 6½x29½ inches.

MATERIALS

⅞ yard of muslin fabric
Scraps of 8 assorted cotton fabrics
10x35-inch piece of batting
1x8 pine board, 29½ inches long
Five 2½-inch Shaker pegs
2 picture hangers
Staple gun and staples
Off-white semigloss latex paint
Wood primer
Drill; ½-inch bit

INSTRUCTIONS

Each Dresden Plate is made of eight fabric wedges of assorted scrap fabrics. Five Dresden Plates are used in our project to obtain the finished size. To adjust the length of the rack, alter the number of plates and cut your board length accordingly.

From muslin, cut one 13x36-inch rectangle for the top and one 16x39-inch piece for backing.

From cardboard, make a template for the small Dresden Plate wedge on page 20.

Draw five wedges on the wrong side of *each* of the eight fabric scraps. Cut out the wedges, adding ¼-inch seam allowances.

To piece the Dresden Plate

Sew together eight wedges, one of each fabric, to form a ring. Sew wedges together on the marked seam lines, leaving the ¼-inch seam allowances unsewn at each end. Press seams to one side.

Turn under the seam allowances on the inner circle and around the outside edges; baste.

For the peg rack

Make five Dresden Plate rings. Center and pin one ring to the 13x36-inch piece of muslin. Pin the remaining rings to each side, spacing them 1 inch apart. Appliqué in place.

Center and layer the top, batting, and backing; baste together.

Hand-quilt each wedge ¼ inch from seams. Then quilt the background in a diagonal grid of 1-inch diamonds.

Trim the excess batting and backing even with the top; overcast-stitch the raw edges.

Draw a ¾-inch-diameter circle in the center of *each* ring. Zigzag-stitch atop the drawn lines. Clip an X inside each stitched circle.

Trim the pine board to 6½-inch width. Center the quilted piece atop the board, taking excess fabric to back side; staple in place.

Prime, then paint, the pegs.

Use ½-inch drill bit to drill ⅝-inch-deep holes in the center of each ring. Glue pegs in holes. Attach picture hangers to the back at both ends.

Bear Sewing Caddy

Shown on page 9.

Finished bear sits 8 inches tall.

MATERIALS

¼ yard of muslin for head, ears, legs, and paws
11x17-inch piece of gold fabric for body bottom and arms
10x10-inch piece of blue fabric for body bodice
Ten 2¾x5-inch assorted fabrics for the skirt
Two ¼-inch-diameter black buttons for eyes
8 inches of pregathered lace, 1¼-inch width
1 yard ¼-inch-wide red ribbon
DMC black pearl cotton (No. 81), 1 skein
Powdered rouge
24 inches of elastic thread
2½-inch-diameter jar lid
Crafts glue
4 small artificial flowers
Polyester fiberfill

continued

INSTRUCTIONS

Note: Sew all seams with right sides facing unless noted otherwise. Use ¼-inch seams throughout. Add ¼-inch seam allowances to all pattern pieces, *right*.

BODY: Cut one 10-inch-diameter circle from gold fabric for body bottom; cut one 9-inch-diameter circle from blue fabric for bodice. Run gathering threads around *each* circle edge. Glue the jar lid in the center of the *bottom* body circle; gather and stuff, leaving a 2-inch-diameter opening.

Gather and stuff bodice circle, leaving a 1½-inch-diameter opening. With the raw edges facing, whipstitch the bodice atop the bottom body, 1 inch from the circle openings.

SKIRT: Sew the long sides of the ten skirt fabrics together to form a tube. To gather top of skirt, turn one edge under 1 inch; press. Machine-zigzag atop elastic thread ½ inch from folded edge. Do not tie elastic.

Turn and press under ¼ inch along bottom of skirt; open the folded edge and run a gathering thread atop the fold line on right side of fabric. Slip the skirt over the body, turn under the bottom fold, gather, and pin the skirt bottom 1¼ inches from the jar lid edge; whipstitch in place. Pull up and tie elastic thread to fit waist.

LEGS: Stitch legs together in pairs, leaving opening for turning. Form toe gusset by matching front and bottom foot seams; sew a straight line across the tip of the toe (forming a small triangle) ¼ inch from corner. Clip curves, turn, stuff, and sew the opening closed. Repeat for other leg. Stitch legs to the sides of body below the skirt hem.

SLEEVES: *Note:* Sleeve pattern is one long piece that fastens to top of bodice, creating both arms.

Stitch paws to ends of sleeves. Stitch sleeves together, leaving center 4 inches unsewn on one side for turning. Clip the curves, turn, and stuff paws only. Run

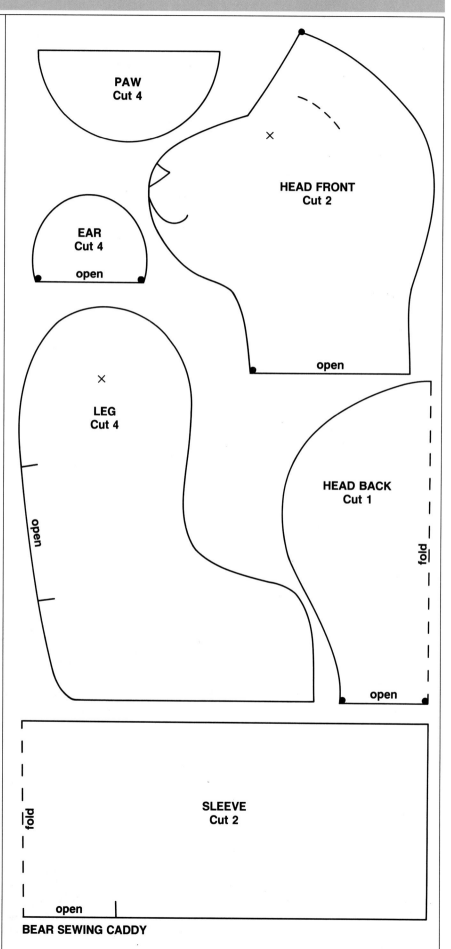

PAW
Cut 4

HEAD FRONT
Cut 2

EAR
Cut 4
open

open

LEG
Cut 4

open

HEAD BACK
Cut 1

fold

open

SLEEVE
Cut 2

fold

open

BEAR SEWING CADDY

gathering thread along the paw seam; pull up and fasten. Stuff sleeve ends, leaving center 4 inches unstuffed; sew opening closed. Pleat the center 2 inches and tack the pleating to top of bodice.

HEAD: Stitch front head seam between dots. Stitch head back to head front. Clip and turn. Baste under ¼ inch at neck opening; stuff head firmly. Satin-stitch the nose and outline-stitch the mouth with pearl cotton. Attach eyes at Xs, as shown on pattern.

Sew ears together in pairs, leaving bottom edges open; turn and stuff lightly. Turn under the raw edges and stitch ears to head. Whipstitch head to body atop the sleeve pleating.

FINISHING: Glue flowers along ear. Add cheeks, using rouge. Cut and stitch lace to fit around neck. Tie one end of ribbon around the bear's neck and one end to a pair of small scissors. Insert notions into gathered skirt to complete.

Pinwheel Tablecloth And Napkins

Shown on pages 10–11.

The finished tablecloth is approximately 47x68½ inches. Napkins are 13 inches square.

MATERIALS
For the tablecloth
1¼ yards *each* of red and green cotton fabric
1 yard of blue cotton fabric
4 yards of yellow cotton fabric
For the set of 4 napkins
1 yard *each* of red, green, yellow, and blue cotton fabrics

INSTRUCTIONS
Note: All cutting measurements include ½-inch seam allowances.

To make the tablecloth
PREPARING THE PATTERNS: Draw the following shapes onto graph or brown paper: The pattern for A, B, and E is a right-angle triangle with 17-inch legs; make one pattern. The pattern for D is a right-angle triangle with 12½-inch legs. Refer to the piecing diagram, *below,* for the dimensions of pattern C.

Make cardboard templates for each of these pattern pieces.

CUTTING THE STRIPS: Cut 5x44-inch strips across the width of the fabrics as follows: 8 *each* from red and green, 6 from blue, and 12 from yellow. The remaining yellow fabric is used for the border and lining.

PIECING THE TRIANGLES: Sew four strips together in the following color sequence to make one strip set: red, green, yellow, and blue. Make five more strip sets. Press seams to one side.

Stack and pin 2 strip sets *right side up* with the red fabric along the *top* edge. Refer to the cutting diagram on page 24, *top,* to make the A triangles. Mark and cut 2 triangles (total of 4) with one leg of template A along the edge of the red strip. Set triangles aside.

continued

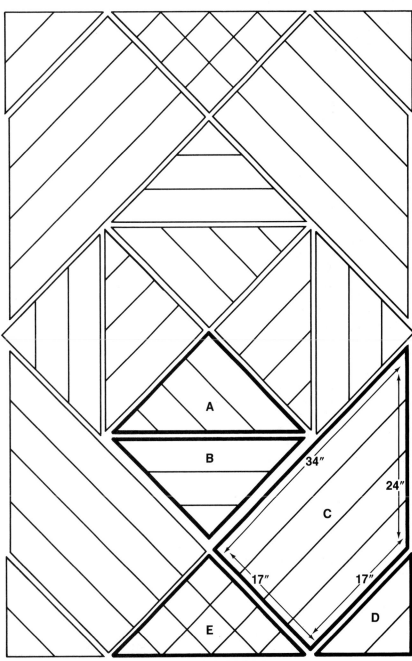

PINWHEEL TABLECLOTH PIECING DIAGRAM

Refer to the cutting diagram to cut the 5-inch-wide rows for the E triangles from the same strip set. You'll have eight strips of varying lengths.

Assemble four of these strip rows as follows referring to the piecing diagram, *center, right,* to prepare the fabric for cutting *one* E triangle: Remove the extra red square from Row 2. Sew this green, yellow, and blue strip to the Row 1 strip.

Remove the red-and-green partial squares from the Row 3 strip. Sew this yellow-and-blue strip to Row 2.

Remove the partial yellow-and-green squares from Row 4. Sew the blue square to Row 3.

Cut an E triangle, placing both legs of template A along the multicolored rows of squares.

Repeat the above assembly instructions to make a second E triangle with remaining four strips.

Stack and pin the remaining four strip sets with two sets *right side up* and two sets *wrong side up.* Lay the strips so the red fabric is along the *top edge.* Mark and cut template C, placing the 34-inch side along the edges of the red strips and the 17-inch side even with the left edges. Cut through all layers to make four pieces.

From the remainder of these four sets, cut the B triangles. Use template A and place the 24-inch side along the blue edges. Cut though all thicknesses to make four triangles.

Stitch the remaining two red and green strips together, pairing a red strip with a green strip. Stack and pin the strip sets *right side up.* Mark and cut two of template D, placing the 17-inch side along the red edges. Cut through both of the thicknesses to make four triangles.

ASSEMBLY: Referring to the piecing diagram on page 23, sew one A triangle to one B triangle to make one square. Make three more squares from the remaining A–B triangles. Then sew these four squares together to make one large center square.

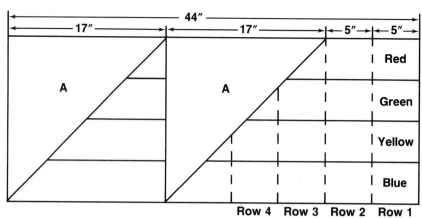

CUTTING DIAGRAM FOR A TRIANGLES AND E ROWS

Sew a D triangle to *each* C piece. Sew one C-D unit to one side of the center square. Sew a second C-D unit to the *opposite* side of the center square.

Sew an E triangle to the two remaining C-D units. Sew these two triangles to opposite sides of the center unit.

Press all seams to one side.

FINISHING: From the remaining yellow fabric, cut a lining piece the same size as the top. Pin lining and top together, wrong sides facing.

To make the borders, sew a 5x44-inch yellow strip to *opposite* short *lining* sides of the cloth, right sides facing. Press under raw edges ½ inch on the long side of the strips. Fold the strip in half and lay the pressed edge atop the sewing line on the right side of the cloth; topstitch in place.

Sew the short ends of *two* yellow strips together. Center and sew this strip to the lining side of the cloth along the long edge. Press under raw edges ½ inch on the long side. Repeat these instructions for the strip on the opposite side.

To finish the corners, fold the border strips in half, right sides facing. Sew short edges together even with the side edges; trim away excesss fabric. Turn strip to right side, lay the pressed edge atop the sewing line on right side of cloth and topstitch in place.

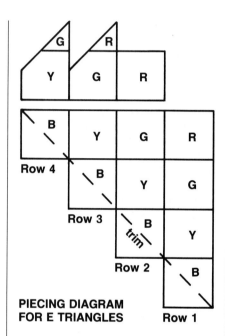

PIECING DIAGRAM FOR E TRIANGLES

Stitch-in-the-ditch around the large center square to keep the layers from shifting.

To make the napkins:

Note: The napkins are assembled as the A triangles on the piecing diagram on page 23. The size of the triangle, however, differs for the napkins. Each napkin has matching color lining and border. Two napkins have blue pinwheels; two napkins have red pinwheels.

PREPARING THE PATTERN: Draw a right-angle triangle with 9-inch legs onto graph paper. Make a cardboard template from this triangle.

CUTTING THE STRIPS: Cut two 3x44-inch strips, two 5x44-inch strips, and a 12-inch square from *each* fabric.

PIECING THE TOPS: Sew the 3x44-inch strips to make two strip sets in the following color sequence: red, green, yellow, and blue.

Pin the two strip sets together, *right sides up*. Mark four triangles, placing one of the 9-inch legs along the edges of the red strips. Then mark four triangles, placing one of the 9-inch legs along the edges of blue strips. Cut out the eight triangles (16 total).

Separate the triangles into two groups of 4 blue-edged triangles and two groups of 4 red-edged triangles before assembly.

To make one napkin, lay out four triangles in one of the groups to form a pinwheel (square). Referring to the piecing diagram on page 23, sew two of these triangles together to make one larger triangle; sew the remaining two together. Then join the two large triangles to form the square.

Repeat these instructions to assemble the remaining three napkins. Press all seams to one side.

FINISHING: Pin *each* napkin top, wrong sides facing, to a 12-inch lining square.

Using the same fabric as the lining for the borders, cut two 5-inch-wide strips to match the length of opposite sides of each napkin. Sew these strips to the lining sides of the napkins, right sides facing. Press under the raw edges ½ inch on the long sides of the strips. Fold the strips in half and lay the pressed edge atop the sewing line on the right side of the nakins; topstitch in place.

Cut remaining strips to match in size the unfinished sides of the napkins plus the seam allowances, and sew in place. Press under raw edges ½ inch on the long side. To finish the corners, fold the strips in half, right sides facing, and sew the short edges together. Turn strips right side out. Lay the pressed edge atop the sewing line on the right side of the napkins; topstitch in place.

Rocky Glen Wall Hanging

Shown on page 12.

The finished wall hanging is 32x34¾ inches.

MATERIALS
9–16 assorted 8x10-inch cotton fabrics in rust, burgundy, and plum color shades
9–16 assorted 9x18-inch cotton fabrics in white, off-white, tan, peach, and mauve
6 small scraps of assorted blue, red, and green fabrics for accent
6–9 assorted 1½-inch-wide strips in shades of burgundy and rust fabrics for border
¼ yard of rust for binding
1¼ yards of muslin for backing
Quilt batting
30-inch-long piece of 1-inch-wide pine lath

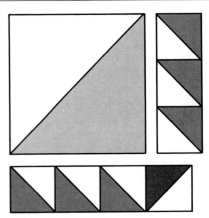

PIECING DIAGRAM

INSTRUCTIONS
Each block is made from five fabric colors. A block is made by piecing a light-colored triangle to a dark-colored triangle. Two sides of this square are bordered with smaller dark and light triangles that differ in shade from the large triangles. The corner square is made from a dark triangle in a third dark shade or an accent color and a light triangle.

continued

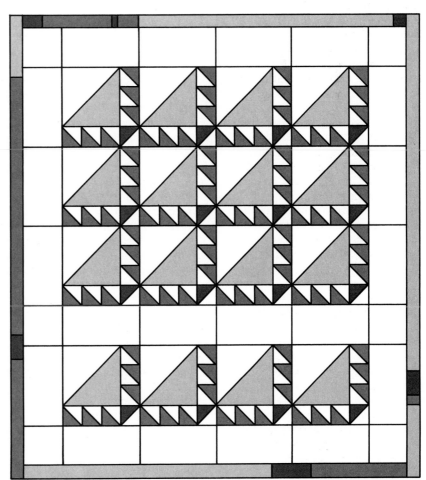

ASSEMBLY DIAGRAM

For a quick and easy method to piece the triangles together, refer to the tip on page 29. The block piecing directions that follow for this project use conventional piecing methods.

Sew all pieces with right sides facing, using ¼-inch seams. The template measurements are given *finished size;* add ¼-inch seam allowances when cutting shapes from fabrics.

PREPARING THE PATTERNS: Using graph paper, draw a 4½-inch right-angle triangle for template A; draw a 1½-inch right-angle triangle for template B; draw a 2¾x6-inch rectangle for template C; and draw a 2¾-inch square for template D. Make cardboard templates for these shapes.

BLOCK PIECING: From one dark fabric, cut one of A; from another dark fabric, cut six of B. Cut one of B from either a dark or accent fabric.

From one light fabric, cut one of A; from another light fabric, cut seven of B.

Referring to the block piecing diagram on page 25, sew the two A triangles together to make a square. Sew the contrasting dark B triangle to a light B triangle to make the corner square. Sew six pairs of dark and light B triangles together to make squares.

Stitch three small squares together; sew this strip to the right side of the large square. Then sew remaining four small squares together, noting the position of the triangles in the corner square. Sew this strip to bottom of the large square to complete block.

PIECING THE TOP: From the assorted light and dark fabrics, cut pieces to make 16 blocks. From remaining asssorted light fabrics, cut 20 of C, and six of D.

Piece together 16 blocks. Referring to the assembly diagram on page 25, sew four blocks together to make one row. Make three more rows. Sew one C piece to the short ends of *each* row.

To make one setting strip, piece the short ends of four assorted C pieces together; sew one D piece to *each* end. Make two more setting strips.

Sew the four rows of blocks together with a setting strip at the top and bottom and between the third and fourth rows.

For the border, cut 1½-inch-wide fabric pieces as follows: Cut 1- and 2-inch lengths from accent fabrics. From the assorted burgundy and rust fabrics, cut random lengths. Using the accent pieces and the assorted randomly cut pieces, piece two strips 30 inches long and two strips 34¾ inches long. In our wall hanging, the accent fabrics are placed about 8 inches from one end of *each* border strip.

Sew the short strips to the top and bottom of the wall hanging. Sew the long strips to the sides.

FINISHING: From the backing fabric, cut a 36x38-inch piece for the back. Layer the top, batting, and backing. Quilt ¼ inch from the seams on the A, C, and D pieces and around the border. When the quilting is completed, trim excess batting and backing.

From the binding fabric, cut four 1½x36-inch strips. Sew the binding, right sides facing, to side edges; trim seams. Turn under ¼ inch on the binding; bring binding to the back and blind-stitch in place. Then sew binding to top and bottom edges in the same manner, carefully finishing the binding corners.

Cut a 6x33-inch strip from the muslin. Press under ¼ inch on long sides. Turn back the short ends 1 inch and machine-stitch in place. Center and hand-sew strip to the top of the wall hanging back just inside the binding seam. Insert 1-inch pine lath inside the strip to hang. For a firmer edge along the bottom, you may wish to make a second casing for a lath insert.

Sunshine and Shadows Piano Bench Cover

Shown on page 13.

The finished size of the pieced cover is 12x40 inches.

MATERIALS
½ yard *each* of peach, light brick red, dark brick red, cranberry, rust, and taupe cotton fabrics
Small scraps of assorted blue, pink, and lavender cotton for accent fabrics
⅝ yard of backing fabric
16x45-inch piece of fleece
12x40-inch piano bench with insert (available through local craft shops or write to: Plain 'n' Fancy, P.O. Box 357, Mathews, VA 23109)

INSTRUCTIONS
PREPARING THE PATTERNS: Draw two 1¼-inch squares onto graph paper. Draw a line diagonally through one of the squares to make two triangles; cut out the shapes. From cardboard, make square and triangle templates.

CUTTING THE PIECES: Cut nine 1¾x34-inch fabric strips as follows: 1 from light brick, and 2 *each* from rust, taupe, dark brick, and peach.

Cut squares as follows, adding ¼-inch seam allowances: 1 from cranberry, 8 from rust, 12 from light brick, 16 from taupe, and 20 *each* from peach and dark brick.

Cut 4 triangles from peach and 4 from accent fabrics, adding ¼-inch seam allowances. Sew the light peach triangles to accent triangles to form squares.

PIECING THE TOP: Using the diagram, *opposite,* piece squares together in nine rows, *each* row containing nine squares. Join the rows to complete the center.

Sew the 34-inch-long strips together, *lengthwise*, in the following color sequence: rust, taupe, dark brick, peach, light brick, peach, dark brick, taupe, and rust. Cut the joined strips into two 17-inch lengths. Sew one short edge of strip set to one side of the center portion; sew the second strip set to the *opposite* side.

To make borders, cut 3½-inch-wide strips in random lengths from assorted reds and accent fabrics. Join strips as desired to make two 45-inch strips; sew the strips to long sides of pieced top.

FINISHING: Layer the top, batting, and backing together. Quilt ⅛ inch from seams on alternate squares and strips and diagonally through the taupe squares.

Staple the cover to the piano bench insert and mount the insert to the bench.

Fast Strip Cutting

Use a rotary cutter for rapid and accurate cutting when your patchwork project requires lots of strips, squares, or rectangles that are the same size. This tool resembles a pizza cutter and, when used with a hard-edge ruler and a cutting mat, it cuts through multiple layers of fabric.

To cut a strip across the width of the fabric, fold the fabric *lengthwise* twice. Lay the fabric on the cutting board and then lay the ruler across the short edge, *perpendicular* to the fold. Roll the cutter away from you to cut and straighten the fabric edge.

Moving across the fabric, aligning the ruler for the strip width, cut the required number of strips. Unroll strips and layer to cut squares or rectangles.

Streak of Lightning Throw and Pillows

Shown on pages 14–15.

Finished size of throw is 36x58½ inches. The large rectanglular pillow is 17x26 inches; the small pillow is 15 inches square.

MATERIALS
For the throw
1 yard of red cotton fabric
½ yard of burgundy cotton fabric
1 yard of black cotton fabric for binding and patchwork
½ yard of green cotton fabric
¾ yard of dark green cotton fabric
1¾ yards of backing fabric
Quilt batting

For the rectangular pillows
½ yard *each* of five assorted cotton fabrics
18x27-inch piece of cotton for *each* pillow back
20x29-inch piece of muslin for *each* top backing
Quilt batting
Polyester fiberfill

For the square pillows
⅓ yard *each* of five assorted cotton fabrics
16-inch square of cotton for *each* pillow back
18-inch square of muslin for *each* top backing
Quilt batting
Polyester fiberfill

INSTRUCTIONS
The throw and pillows are composed of triangles that are sewn together to form squares. The position of the squares creates the zigzag or Streak of Lightning quilt pattern.

PREPARING THE PATTERN: Draw a 4½-inch square onto graph paper. Draw a diagonal line across the square to make the triangle pattern. Make a cardboard template from the triangle; add ¼-inch seam allowances to all sides of triangle.

continued

E	B	D	F	E	F	D	B	E
B	D	F	E	D	E	F	D	B
D	F	E	D	C	D	E	F	D
F	E	D	C	B	C	D	E	F
E	D	C	B	A	B	C	D	E
F	E	D	C	B	C	D	E	F
D	F	E	D	C	D	E	F	D
B	D	F	E	D	E	F	D	B
E	B	D	F	E	F	D	B	E

ASSEMBLY DIAGRAM

COLOR KEY
A Cranberry   D Peach
B Light Brick Red   E Dark Brick Red
C Rust   F Taupe

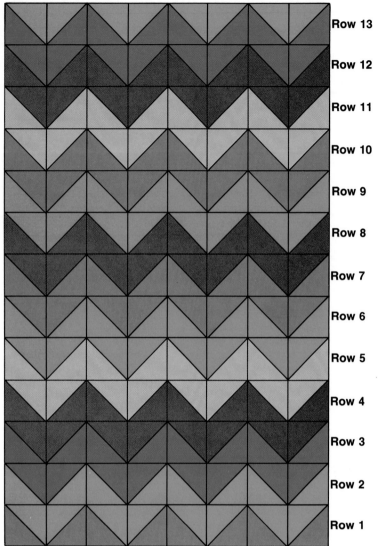

STREAK OF LIGHTNING THROW

Row 13
Row 12
Row 11
Row 10
Row 9
Row 8
Row 7
Row 6
Row 5
Row 4
Row 3
Row 2
Row 1

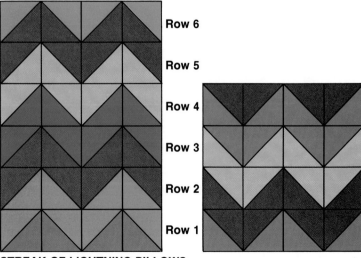

STREAK OF LIGHTNING PILLOWS

Row 6
Row 5
Row 4
Row 3
Row 2
Row 1

For the throw

The throw top is assembled by sewing thirteen strips of assembled squares together. Each strip has eight squares.

CUTTING THE PIECES: Cut the triangles as follows: cut 56 from red fabric, cut 48 from black fabric, cut 40 from dark green fabric, and cut 32 *each* from the burgundy and green fabrics.

ASSEMBLY OF TOP: Piece eight red triangles to eight dark green triangles to assemble eight squares. Beginning at the bottom left corner and referring to the diagram, *top, left,* for color placements, sew these eight squares together to form one row. For the second row, piece red and burgundy triangles together. Continue in this manner until the 13 rows are assembled. Sew the thirteen rows together to complete the top.

FINISHING: Cut backing and batting slightly larger than the quilt top. Then layer the backing, batting, and top; baste together. Hand-quilt following the Streak of Lightning pattern, spacing quilting lines 1 inch apart. Trim away excess batting and backing.

For the binding, cut five 1½-inch-wide strips across the fabric width from the black fabric; piece strips. With right sides together, sew binding to right side of quilt top. Fold binding to back side, turn under seam allowance, and hand-sew in place.

For the rectangular pillows

Using colors of your choice, refer to the photograph on page 14 as a guide. For example, one pillow can be made from just three fabric colors.

One large pillow top is assembled by sewing six strips of assembled squares together. Each strip has four squares.

CUTTING THE PIECES: Cut 48 triangles of assorted fabrics to form the Streak of Lightning design. Use colors of your choice, or refer to the pillow piecing diagrams, *opposite,* to determine the number of triangles that are cut from each fabric.

ASSEMBLY OF TOP: To complete Row 1, sew eight triangles into four squares; piece these squares together to make one strip. Assemble five more strips. Sew strips together to form the pillow top.

FINISHING: Layer the muslin backing, batting, and top; baste together. Hand- or machine-quilt following the Streak of Lightning pattern, spacing the quilting lines 1 inch apart. Trim away excess batting and backing.

Sew pillow top to pillow back, using ½-inch seams; leave opening for turning. Clip the corners, turn, and stuff. Sew the opening closed.

For the square pillow

Pillow top is assembled by sewing four strips of joined squares together. Each strip contains four squares.

CUTTING THE PIECES: Cut 32 triangles of assorted fabrics to form the Streak of Lightning design. Use colors of your choice, or refer to the piecing diagram, *left, center,* to determine the number of triangles that are cut from each fabric.

ASSEMBLY OF TOP: To complete Row 1, piece eight triangles into four squares; sew squares together to make one strip. Assemble three more strips. Sew the strips together to form pillow top.

FINISHING: Center and layer the muslin backing, batting, and top; baste together. Hand- or machine-quilt, following the Streak of Lightning pattern, spacing the quilting lines 1 inch apart.

Trim edges evenly on all sides so pillow top is 16 inches square. Sew pillow top to backing using ½-inch seams; leave opening for turning. Clip corners, turn, and stuff. Sew the opening closed.

Quick and Easy Method for Piecing Patchwork Triangles

When your patchwork requires lots of equal squares made from two right-angle triangles, use the quick-piecing method, *below,* to save time and speed the assembly of these units.

The Streak of Lightning throw and pillows, pages 14 and 15, the Rocky Glen wall hanging, page 12, and the Delectable Mountains quilt, page 61, are examples of projects in this book that lend themselves to this timesaving piecing.

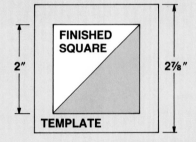

1. First, determine the *finished* size of the square that two assembled right-angle triangles make. Add ⅞ inch to this square to allow for the ¼-inch seam allowances. For example, if you need a finished 2-inch square, make a 2⅞-inch-square template.

Cut half the number of squares from *each* of the dark and light fabrics that the instructions cite for cutting right-angle triangles. For example, if pattern directions call for 32 *each* dark and light right-angle triangles, cut 16 *each* dark and light squares.

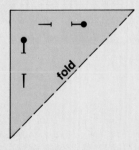

2. Place one dark and one light square together, right sides facing; pin them together in each side. Fold the squares in half, *diagonally;* press crease lightly.

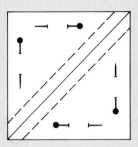

3. Unfold the square. Using the crease as a guide, stitch two diagonal lines ¼ inch beyond the crease through both thicknesses.

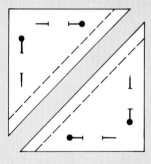

4. Cut the squares apart through the crease line.

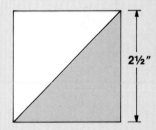

5. Unfold the two triangles. You have two squares, *each* with one light and one dark right-angle triangle. These assembled squares are ½ inch larger than the finished size. Assemble the squares using ¼-inch seams. Always press the seams toward the darker fabric. Repeat steps 2–5 to complete the required number of squares.

FAVORITE PIECED QUILTS

SOFT AND PRETTY

If you're a scrap saver, the quilt here and those on the next two pages are for you. These three quilts are exquisite examples of patchwork designs that make the most of your fabric snips.

The popular Trip Around the World quilt here is visually striking and easy to piece. The interplay of tiny prints and solid pastels creates a freshness that is typical of quilts made in the 1930s.

Lavender, green, pink, blue, and yellow 2-inch fabric squares, pieced on the diagonal, create this 87x98-inch Around the World quilt.

The sawtooth edges are rectangles, folded into squares and assembled into the quilt as you work the diagonal piecing.

When you work this design in alternating colors of dark and light fabrics, you create the Sunshine and Shadow pattern, characteristic of Pennsylvania Amish quilts.

How-to instructions begin on page 34.

The pastel hexagon flowers, pieced with green diamond paths along the white borders of the blossoms, make the Grandmother's Flower Garden quilt, *above,* spectacular.

Use the tiniest of your fabric scraps to make this 82x92-inch quilt. Simply coordinate your prints and solids to make each of the 46 center flower blocks and the 6 partial blocks along the short sides.

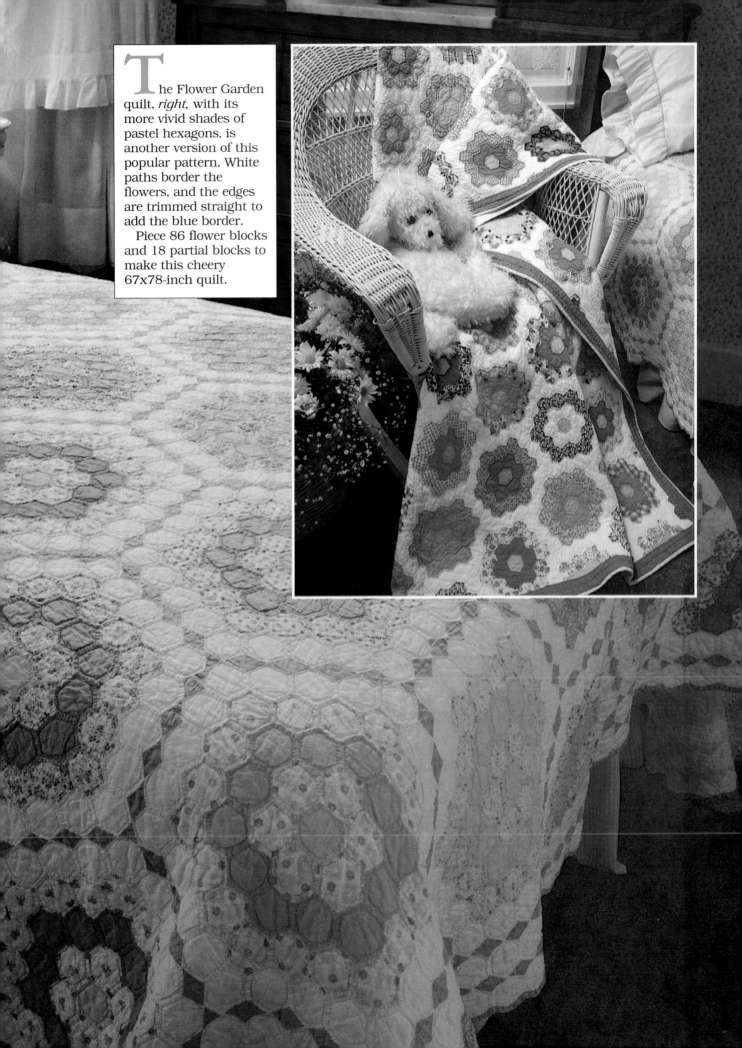

T he Flower Garden quilt, *right,* with its more vivid shades of pastel hexagons, is another version of this popular pattern. White paths border the flowers, and the edges are trimmed straight to add the blue border.

Piece 86 flower blocks and 18 partial blocks to make this cheery 67x78-inch quilt.

Trip Around the World Quilt

Shown on pages 30–31.

Finished size of quilt is approximately 87x98 inches.

MATERIALS

Solid pastel 44-inch-wide fabrics in the following amounts: 9 yards of yellow for the backing and patchwork pieces, ¼ yard of light green, ¾ yard of lavender, ¼ yard of bright blue, 1 yard of pink, ½ yard of bright green, ½ yard of light blue

Two *each* print fabrics to coordinate with solid-color fabrics as follows: ½ yard of *each* yellow print, ¼ yard of *each* light green print, ¾ yard of *each* lavender print, ⅓ yard of *each* bright blue print, 1 yard of *each* pink print, ½ yard of *each* bright green print, ¾ yard of *each* light blue print

Quilt batting

INSTRUCTIONS

The center of the quilt is composed of 2-inch squares pieced on the diagonal into strips. The border units are 2x4-inch rectangles sewn into squares. The strips are then joined to complete the top of the quilt.

PREPARING THE PATTERNS: To make the templates, draw a 2½-inch square and a 2½x4½-inch rectangle onto graph paper; cut out shapes. Trace around shapes onto cardboard or plastic; cut out. Templates include ¼-inch seam allowances.

CUTTING THE PIECES: From solid-yellow fabric, cut *two* 3-yard 44-inch-wide pieces and one 3-yard 12-inch-wide piece for the backing; set aside. From solid-yellow fabric, cut 73 squares and 128 rectangles (for the A rows on the diagram, *right*). From one yellow print, cut 84 squares (B rows). From other yellow print cut 92 squares (C rows).

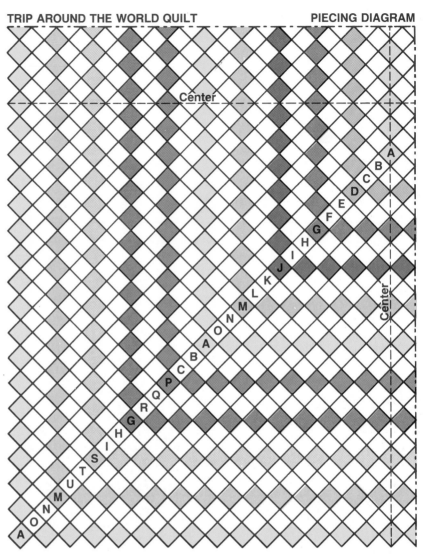

TRIP AROUND THE WORLD QUILT   PIECING DIAGRAM

From light green fabric, cut 20 squares (D row). From one light green print, cut 24 squares (E row). From the other light green print, cut 28 squares (F row).

From lavender fabric, cut 124 squares (G rows). From one of the lavender prints, cut 132 squares (H rows). From other lavender print, cut 140 squares (I rows).

From the bright blue, cut 44 squares (J row). From one of the bright blue prints, cut 48 squares (K row). From other bright blue print, cut 52 squares (L row).

From pink, cut 172 squares (M rows). From one pink print, cut 180 squares (N rows). From the other pink print, cut 188 squares (O rows).

From bright green fabric, cut 80 squares (P row). From one of the bright green prints, cut 84 squares (Q row). From the other

bright green print, cut 88 squares (R row).

From light blue fabric, cut 104 squares (S row). From one light blue print, cut 108 squares (T row). From the second light blue print, cut 112 squares (U row).

PIECING: Begin by preparing the border pieces. Fold the yellow rectangles in half, right sides facing. Sew along *one* side adjacent to the folded edge on *each* of the 124 rectangles. For the four corner rectangles, sew along *both* sides adjacent to the folded edge. Turn pieces and press.

For ease in assembly, draw the complete quilt pattern onto graph paper. Working diagonally from lower left corner of your drawing, piece the squares into strips, using ¼-inch seams. Strips begin and end with a yellow border square. Sew strips together to complete quilt top.

ASSEMBLY: Sew three backing pieces together, positioning the 12-inch piece in the center. Trim piece to measure 2 inches beyond the assembled pieced top. Cut batting to match. Sandwich the batting between the top and backing pieces; baste together.

QUILTING: Quilt diagonal lines across the center of the squares. Then repeat the diagonal quilting in the opposite direction. Do not quilt the border squares.

FINISHING: Trim away excess batting. Then trim away excess backing to within ¼ inch of the *center* of the yellow border pieces. Turn under ¼ inch and hand-sew in place.

Green Path Flower Garden Quilt

Shown on pages 32–33.

Finished size of quilt is approximately 82x92 inches.

MATERIALS
½ yard of solid-yellow fabric for flower centers and second row of flower petals

¼ yard *each* of solid-pastel fabrics in the following colors: green, pink, lavender, peach, orange, blue, and rose for second row of flower petals

Scraps of assorted print pastel fabrics to coordinate with the solid-pastel fabric for the first and third row of flower petals (enough of 1 fabric to cut 24 hexagons for one flower)

4¾ yards of white cotton fabric for the hexagons, triangles, and parallelograms

3½ yards of light green fabric for the paths and bias binding.

6 yards of white cotton fabric for the backing

Quilt batting

continued

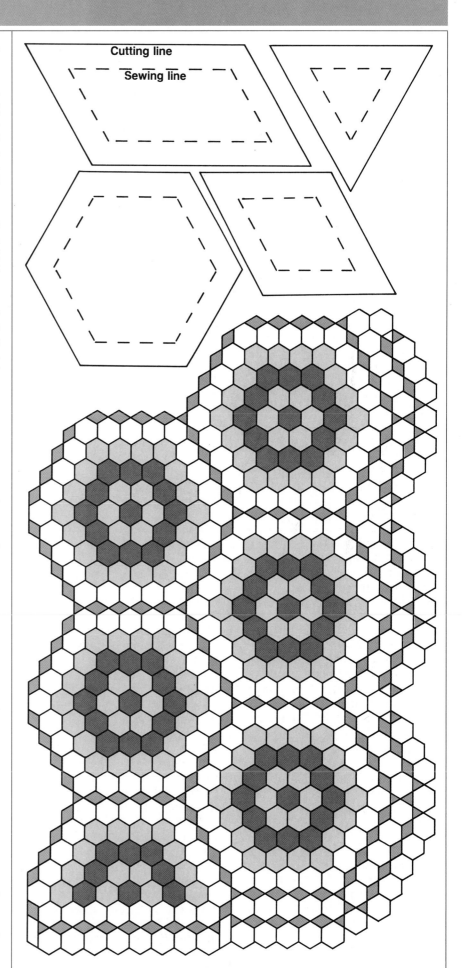

FAVORITE PIECED QUILTS

INSTRUCTIONS

The center of the pieced top consists of 46 flower blocks. Each *block* is made by joining 61 individual hexagons as follows: 1 yellow for center, 24 pastel print hexagons for the first and third rows of flower petals, 12 solid pastel hexagons for second row of petals, and 24 white hexagons for the borders around the flowers.

Along the short sides are 6 partial flowers that consist of one center hexagon, 14 pastel print hexagons for the first and third rows of petals, 7 solid-color hexagons for the second row of petals, and 13 white hexagons for the borders.

A single row of diamond green paths circles the flowers and a double row of green paths completes its border.

Carefully trace the *cutting line* hexagon, triangle, diamond, and parallelogram on page 35 onto cardboard or a plastic lid; cut out. Next, trace the *seam line* of these shapes and cut templates for marking the stitching lines. (To ensure accurate piecing, replace templates as they become worn).

Beginning with the cutting line template, trace hexagons on the wrong side of each fabric. Always place the templates on the fabric so that two parallel sides of the hexagon are aligned along the horizontal or vertical grain line of the fabric. Then center the seam line template inside the larger hexagon and trace around it.

Cut hexagons from the fabrics as follows: Cut 52 hexagons from yellow for centers. Cut 594 assorted solid-color hexagons for the second row of petals. Cut these in multiples of 12 (the same color) for the 46 center flowers and in multiples of 7 for the 6 border flowers.

Cut 1,188 assorted print color hexagons for the first and third rows of petals. Cut these in multiples of 24 for the center flowers and in multiples of 14 for the border flowers. When cutting from the print fabrics, you may want to center a flower on some of these hexagons. This is an attractive way to use the fabric.

From the white fabric, trace and cut 12 parallelograms and 24 triangles. Cut 1,608 white hexagons for paths on the 52 center blocks. More white hexagons will be needed for the border after the center blocks and partial flowers are sewn together.

From green, cut 834 diamonds and 222 triangles.

For ease in assembly, stack the hexagons for *each* flower and hold them together on a knotted strand of thread.

BLOCK PIECING: Referring to the diagram on page 35, piece the flower blocks as follows: Sew one of the print hexagon sides to the yellow center hexagon, right sides together. Stitch from seam line to seam line, leaving seam allowances free. Continue to add hexagons until the first row of petals is complete. Press seams *around* the circle to one side and seams at *top* of yellow hexagon toward the center. Add the second and third rows of petals, pressing the seams as each row is completed. Then add 24 muslin hexagons to outer edge of each flower.

Piece the partial flowers blocks together in the same manner, referring to the diagram on page 35.

ASSEMBLY: Join the 46 blocks by adding the green diamonds and triangles between the flower blocks. There will be four rows with 7 blocks and three rows with 6 blocks. Then add the 3 partial flowers to *each* of top and bottom edges. Follow the piecing diagram on page 35 to add the border. Note the position of the parallelograms and small triangles as you add the border to the partial-flower sides.

FINISHING: Cut backing and batting materials 2 inches larger than quilt top. Sandwich batting between the top and backing and baste together. Quilt ¼ inch inside the seam lines of each hexagon shape.

Trim backing and batting even with quilt top. Make bias binding from the green fabric and bind quilt; sew the binding along the quilt edges to shape the scallops.

Grandmother's Flower Garden Quilt

Shown on page 33.

The quilt shown measures 67x78 inches.

MATERIALS
2¼ yards of medium blue fabric for unpieced borders and solid-color petals
⅓ yard of yellow fabric for flower centers
¼ yard of 8 or more solid-color pastel fabrics for first-circle petals
½ yard of 8 or more pastel prints for second-circle petals
3½ yards of white cotton fabric for the path between the flowers
5 yards *each* of off-white cotton fabric for backing fabric
Quilt batting

INSTRUCTIONS
The center of the pieced top consists of 86 blocks. Each *block* is made by joining 28 individual hexagons as follows: 1 yellow for center, 6 solid pastel fabric for first row of petals, 12 pastel print fabric for second row of petals, and 8 white hexagons for the path.

Along the outside long edges are 18 partial flowers that consist of one center hexagon, four hexagons for the first row of petals, and seven hexagons for the second row of petals. Along the top and bottom edges, white hexagons are joined to straighten the edges. When the border is added, it will cut off some of the hexagons, squaring off the quilt, to obtain the finished size.

Carefully trace the *cutting line* hexagon pattern on page 37, onto cardboard or plastic lid; cut out. Next, trace *seam line* of hexagon pattern and cut another template for marking the stitching lines. (For accurate piecing, replace templates as they become worn.)

Beginning with the cutting line template, trace hexagons on the wrong side of each fabric. Always place the templates on the fabric so that two parallel sides of the hexagon are aligned along the horizontal or vertical grain line of the fabric. Then center the seamline template inside the larger hexagon and trace around it.

Cut hexagons from the fabrics as follows: Cut 104 hexagons from yellow for centers. Cut 588 assorted solid-color hexagons for the first row of petals. Cut these in multiples of 6 (the same color) for the 86 center flowers and in multiples of 4 for the 18 border flowers. Cut 1,158 assorted print color hexagons for the second row of petals. Cut these in multiples of 12 for the center flowers and in multiples of 7 for the border flowers.

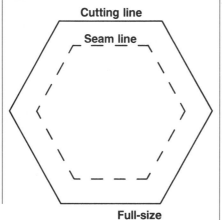

Cutting line

Seam line

Full-size

Cut 688 white hexagons for the paths on the 86 center blocks. Then cut additional white hexagons as needed to square off the top and bottom edges after the center blocks and partial flowers are pieced together.

For ease in assembly, stack the hexagons for *each* of the flowers and hold them together on a knotted strand of thread.

BLOCK PIECING: Refer to the diagram, *left*, to piece the flower blocks as follows: Sew one of the solid-color sides to the yellow center hexagon, right sides together. Stitch from seam line to seam line, leaving the seam allowances free. Continue to add hexagons until the first circle of petals is complete. Press seams *around* the circle to one side; press seams at *top* of yellow hexagon toward the center of the flower. Add the second row of petals to the first row of petals and press seams. Then add 8 muslin hexagons to outer edge of each flower.

Piece the partial flowers together in the same manner, referring to the diagram, *left*.

ASSEMBLY: Piece together the 86 center blocks. There will be five rows with 10 blocks and 4 rows with 9 blocks. Then add nine partial flowers to *each* of the side edges. Fill in top and bottom edges of quilt with white hexagons to square off the top.

From the blue fabric, cut two 2½-inch-wide strips to measure length of quilt. Stitch borders to sides using ¼-inch seams. When borders are added, they will cut off the edge hexagons, squaring off the quilt. Cut 2½-inch top and bottom borders and sew in place.

FINISHING: Cut backing and batting 2 inches larger than quilt top. Layer batting between top and backing and baste together. Quilt ¼ inch inside the seam lines of hexagon shapes and through the center of borders.

Cut away excess batting. Trim backing, leaving 1 inch around all sides. Press backing forward ¼ inch and fold it to front atop the border seamline; sew it in place.

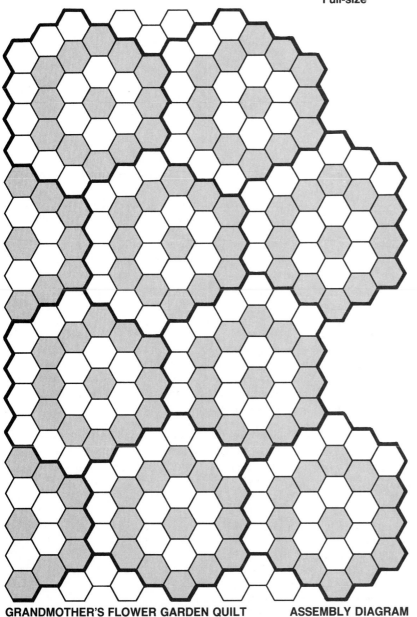

GRANDMOTHER'S FLOWER GARDEN QUILT   **ASSEMBLY DIAGRAM**

PLAYFUL PATTERNS

TO CRAFT
FOR KIDS

Want to make your kids' rooms look great and at the same time be a place they'll love to call their own? Featured here and on the next six pages are lively patchwork projects for a special little miss or a bright young aviator. Adapt one or all of these ideas for wonderful small-folk bedroom accessories.

The charming old-world moppets, dancing in a bed of flowers with roaming chicks on the curtain, *opposite*, inspired the many patchwork uses in this cheerful, sunny room.

For a delicate and airy look, machine-appliqué these pastel motifs onto a 54-inch-wide sheer fabric. To ensure that the curtain fits your window, determine the fabric yardage you need to buy. Calculate the length of your window, then add to it the length of the hems along the top and bottom edges.

The 13-inch throw pillows, plus their 3½-inch-wide ruffles, are fun and easy ways to use your fabric scraps.

Use the tulip motif on a background of striped fabric blocks to create the pillow, *far right,* or use the rose design in a circular arrangement on a plain fabric to make the pillow, *right*.

The how-to instructions for the projects in this chapter begin on page 46.

Imagine the sweet dreams in this so-adorable bed! We used purchased bed linens—sheets, sham, and dust ruffle—to take the chore out of making the soft sleeping accessories, *left*.

The dancing folk, flanked by tulips, adorn the sham. Rip out three sides of a purchased sham to make the machine-appliquéing easy. When all the embellishments are complete, resew the seams.

Tulips and roses grow in a row along the edge of the dust ruffle. Baby chicks, in groups of two and three, strut across the top sheet.

Enlist the woodworker in your house to complete this fanciful decor with the matching headboard.

Use the motifs to bedeck a board that fits a twin-size Hollywood frame. Cut this headboard from ¾-inch particleboard or plywood and the motifs from ¼-inch tempered hardboard. Paint the figures with acrylic paints that match the fabric colors.

If you want to please all the little children in your house, then stitch the bright yellow chicks that hunt and peck across the sheet and pillowcase, *below*. For a more varied color scheme, use lots of scrap colors to make linens kids will love.

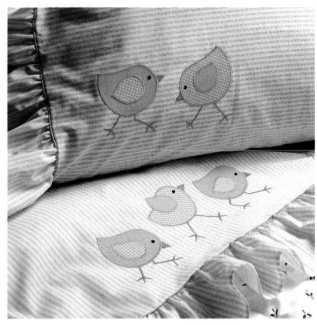

PLAYFUL PATTERNS

The lofty notions of the young aviator in your house will soar in this red, white, and blue room full of airborne accessories.

Piece the 64½x79½-inch twin-bed-size airplane quilt, *opposite,* for openers. Bright blue airplanes, pieced into 7½-inch white squares that resemble clouds, alternate with lighter blue blocks for the sky. A 6-inch blue border completes the quilt top.

The oversize sham (it fits a king-size pillow) features colorful machine-appliqué planes on a 6-inch white fabric strip.

Bands of blue and white squares, fashioned in a checkered arrangement, border the flying planes. Bright red pipings define the segments and finish the edges of the pillow top.

For a window treatment without frills and ruffles, cross-stitch the airplane motif onto panels of 11-count Aida cloth.

Purchase shutters that come with an opening for a fabric insert. When the cross-stitching is complete, fasten the stitcheries to the insert panels and tack in place.

PLAYFUL PATTERNS

All junior pilots will love the soft airplane toy, *opposite*. It's a teaching toy, with a propeller that snaps on and off, wings that tie on with ribbons, and a tail trimmed with felt circles that button.

To give your pilot a more pleasant ride, stitch the brightly colored throw pillows, decorated with machine-appliqué planes. When it's time for refueling, your young aviator will rest comfortably in his aircraft cabin of fanciful flight details.

The blue and white stenciled bulletin board, *below,* with its Shaker pegs, is a perfect place to display or hang all the treasures of a would-be birdman.

Constructed from 1x6-inch pine boards, its outside dimensions are 30½x31½ inches. The boards are trimmed to make a 5-inch-wide frame. Use the full-size airplane quilt motif to make your stencil pattern. Select a fiberboard of your choice for the bulletin board insert.

PLAYFUL PATTERNS

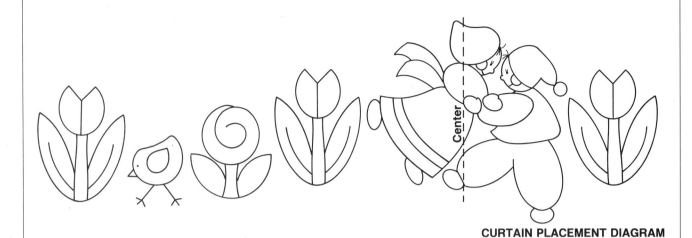

CURTAIN PLACEMENT DIAGRAM

Appliqué Curtain

Shown on page 39.

Finished width of curtain is 54 inches.

MATERIALS
Sheer white fabric, 60 inches
 wide, length to fit window
 plus hems
¼ yard of green cotton fabric
⅛ yard *each* of solid yellow,
 pink, lavender, blue, and rose
 cotton fabrics
Scraps of striped and pindot
 blue cotton fabrics and striped
 pink cotton fabric
Scraps of yellow gingham,
 bright yellow, and peach
 cotton fabrics
Threads to match appliqué
 fabrics
Fusible webbing, or paper-
 backed fusible webbing
Pink and black embroidery floss
Scraps of yellow yarn for hair

INSTRUCTIONS
 PREPARING THE PATTERNS:
Trace the full-size patterns (flowers, *opposite,* chick on page 50,
and the dancing boy and girl on
pages 48 and 49) onto tracing paper. Cut out shapes. Then cut out
the parts of each motif to make
the appliqué patterns. The heavy
lines around the shapes indicate
patterns. Make cardboard templates for *each* of the patterns.

CUTTING THE PIECES: If you
use the paper-backed fusible
webbing for appliqué assembly,
press this webbing to the appliqué fabrics *before you draw and
cut out the pieces.*
 Draw the patterns as follows
atop the *right* sides of fabrics: For
all the flowers, draw two lavender
and two yellow tulips, two pink
roses, four green tulip stems and
leaves, and two green rose stems
and leaves. Draw the stitching details of the flowers and leaves atop
the pieces.
 For the chicks, cut two yellow
bodies, two bright yellow beaks,
and two yellow gingham wings.
 For the girl, from rose, cut skirt
and bandanna; from pink, cut
two feet, a cheek, and a dress tie;
from striped pink, cut the sleeve
and skirt trim; from peach, cut a
hand and face.
 For the boy, from blue, cut the
pants, a sleeve, and a hat tassel;
from the blue stripe, cut shirt
bodice; from the blue pindot, cut
hat and shoes.
 Cut matching shapes for all
pieces from fusible webbing if
you are not using paper-backed
fusible webbing.

 ASSSEMBLY: Draw a straight
line 8½ inches from the bottom
edge of the curtain fabric with the
water-erasable pen. Our curtain
has a 2½-inch hem that is turned
under twice. Using the diagram,
above, for placement, lay the motifs atop the fabric and fuse in
place. Machine-zigzag around the

shapes and stitch the details with
matching threads.
 Draw the legs and feet of the
chicks beneath their bodies and
stitch atop the curtain fabric. Add
black satin-stitch eyes to children
and chicks. With pink floss, outline-stitch the children's mouths.

 FINISHING: Hem bottom and
sides of curtain, turning edge under twice for better stability. Finish top of curtain as desired.

Appliqué Throw Pillows

Shown on pages 38–39.

Finished square pillow is 13 inches; the finished round pillow is 13
inches in diameter. The measurements do not include the 3½-
inch-wide ruffles.

MATERIALS
For both pillows
Polyester fiberfill
Threads to match fabric colors
Fusible webbing, or paper-
 backed fusible webbing
Water-erasable pen
For the square pillow
1 yard of white-and-pink print
 cotton fabric
½ yard of pink-and-white
 striped cotton fabric
¼ yard of green cotton fabric
Scrap of lavender cotton fabric
1½ yards of cotton cording

For the round pillow

1 yard of pink-and-white striped
   cotton fabric
½ yard of white cotton fabric
Scraps of solid pink, rose, and
   green cotton fabrics
1½ yards of cotton cording

INSTRUCTIONS

PREPARING THE PATTERNS:
Trace the full-size patterns (flowers and stems), *opposite* and *below,* onto tracing paper. Cut out shapes. Then cut out the parts of each motif to make the appliqué patterns. Heavy lines around the shapes indicate patterns. Make cardboard templates for *each* of the patterns.

To make the square pillow

CUTTING THE PIECES: *Note:* If you use the paper-backed fusible webbing for appliqué assembly, press this webbing to appliqué fabrics *before you draw and cut out the pieces.*

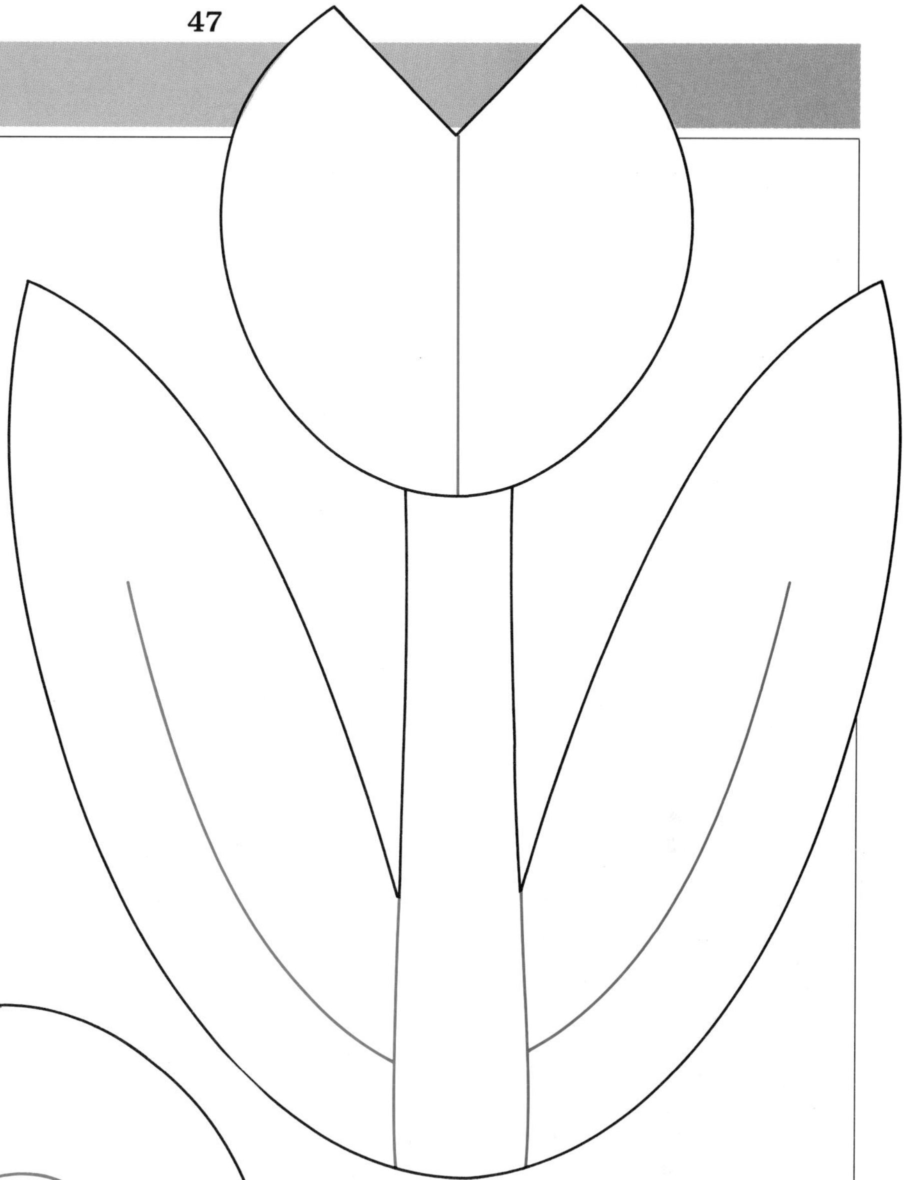

Draw the patterns atop *right* sides of fabrics as follows: Draw one lavender tulip and one green stem and leaves. With the water-erasable pen, draw the stitching details of the flowers and leaves atop the pieces.

Cut matching shapes for all of the pieces from the fusible webbing if you are not using the paper-backed webbing.

Draw a 5½-inch square onto graph paper. Make a cardboard template. From striped fabric, cut four squares with a pink stripe running diagonally through center of *each* square. From remaining striped fabric, cut and piece 1-inch-wide bias strips to measure 54 inches to cover the cording.

From the green fabric, cut two strips, *each* 2x10½ inches, and two strips, *each* 2x13½ inches.

continued

CUTTING LINE ———
STITCH DETAIL ___

PLAYFUL PATTERNS

Center

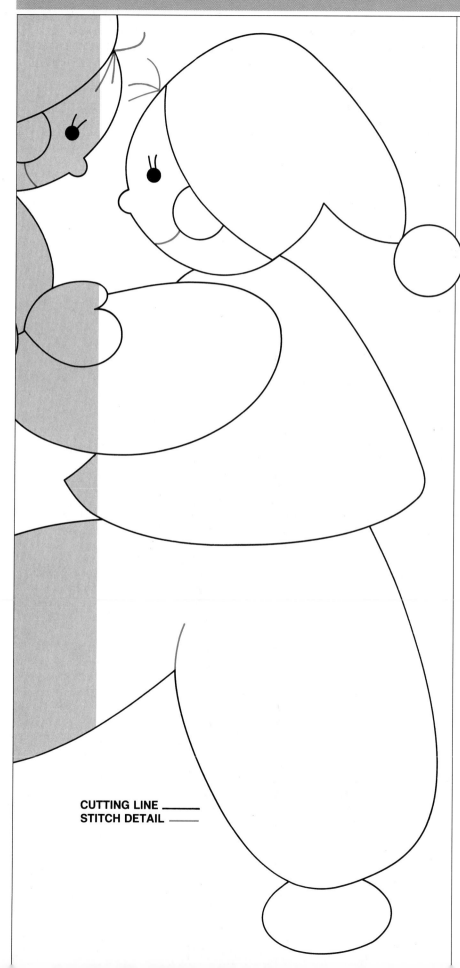

CUTTING LINE ——————
STITCH DETAIL ——————

From the white-and-pink print fabric, cut two 8x44-inch strips for the ruffle. Cut a 13½-inch square for the pillow back.

ASSEMBLY: Use ¼-inch seam allowances to piece the striped squares together to form a large square, positioning the squares so the stripes form a square (see photo on page 39).

Center the tulip motif (stem and flower) atop the fabric, positioning the stem bottom 1 inch from the raw edge. Fuse in place; then machine-zigzag with matching threads around the shapes and details

Sew the two short green strips to pillow top and bottom; sew the long green strips to pillow sides.

FINISHING: Cover the cording with the 54-inch bias strip to make piping. Sew piping to pillow top, right sides facing.

Join the short ends of the ruffle strips into a loop. Fold the ruffle in half, wrong sides together and raw edges even. Run gathering threads ¼ inch from raw edge. Gather to fit pillow top; sew ruffle atop piping seam line.

Sew pillow top to pillow back, right sides together, leaving an opening for turning. Clip corners, turn, stuff, and sew the opening closed.

To make the round pillow

CUTTING THE PIECES: Draw two pink roses, two rose-colored roses, and four green stems and leaves. Cut matching shapes from the fusible webbing if you are not using the paper backed webbing.

Cut two 13½-inch-diameter circles from the white fabric for the pillow front and back.

From the striped fabric, cut two 8x44-inch strips for the ruffle. From the remaining striped fabric, cut and piece the 1-inch-wide bias strips to cover the cording.

ASSEMBLY: Fold pillow front circle in fourths; press lightly atop folds. Unfold circle. Position a rose stem atop *each* of the folded edges, with the bottom edges 1
continued

inch from the raw edge; fuse in place. Fuse roses atop each stem, placing the colors opposite each other. Machine-zigzag around the shapes and their details with matching threads.

FINISHING: To complete, follow the finishing instructions for the square pillow on page 49.

Appliquéd Nightshirt

Shown on page 39.

MATERIALS
Commercial nightshirt pattern
Blue gingham cotton for shirt front and back (yardage as specified in pattern)
Blue striped cotton for sleeves, tab and pocket (yardage as specified in pattern)
Pregathered ½-inch-wide lace trim
White buttons
Scraps of yellow gingham, solid yellow, and golden yellow cotton fabrics for chick appliqués
Threads to match appliqué fabrics
Black embroidery floss for chick's eye
Fusible webbing or paper-backed fusible webbing

INSTRUCTIONS
Assemble nightshirt following the pattern directions, adding the lace trim to neck and tab front.

APPLIQUÉING THE POCKET: Trace the full-size pattern for the chick, *below,* onto tracing paper. Cut out shape. Then cut out the parts to make the appliqué patterns. The heavy lines around the shapes indicate the patterns. Make cardboard templates for all the patterns.
Note: If you use paper-backed fusible webbing for appliqué assembly, press this webbing to the appliqué fabrics *before you draw and cut out the pieces.*
Draw and cut one yellow body, one golden yellow beak, and one yellow gingham wing.
Cut matching shapes for all of the pieces from the fusible webbing if you are not using paper-backed webbing.
Center and fuse the chick to the pocket. Machine-zigzag around shapes with matching threads. Draw the legs and feet of the chick beneath the body and stitch atop the pocket fabric. Add black satin-stitch eye.
Sew pocket to shirt.

Wood Appliqué Headboard

Shown on page 40.

Our headboard is designed to fit and bolt onto a twin-size Hollywood frame. It is 43 inches tall and 39 inches wide.

MATERIALS
39x43 inches of ¾-inch particleboard or plywood
Scraps of ¼-inch tempered hardboard
White primer
Acrylic paints in the following colors: yellow, lavender, pink, rose, blue, green, white, light and dark blue, and peach
Carpenter's glue
Graphite paper
Clear spray varnish
Semigloss pink tinted white latex paint
Four ¼x1¼-inch carriage bolts, nuts, and washers

INSTRUCTIONS
PREPARING THE PATTERNS: Trace onto tracing paper the full-size patterns of the flowers on page 47 to include the stems and leaves, and the dancing boy and girl on pages 48–49 as a single unit; cut out.

FOR THE WOOD APPLIQUÉ MOTIFS: Trace two *each* tulip and rose patterns onto the hardboard; cut out. Trace the boy and girl unit onto the hardboard and cut out.
Round the edges of the pieces with a fine wood rasp. Sand all edges smooth.
Prime the top and side edges of all pieces. Using graphite paper, draw the details of the children atop the pieces. Referring to the photograph on page 40, paint the details. When the paint is dry, spray all pieces with a light coat of varnish.

CUTTING THE HEADBOARD: Lay the particleboard in a horizontal position. Then place the appliqué pieces atop the particleboard. Center the boy and girl, and space the flowers in a curved

CUTTING LINE ⎯⎯⎯⎯
STITCH DETAIL ⎯ ⎯ ⎯

line. The top of the girl's hat is 3 inches from the top edge of the board. (Use double-face tape to hold them in place.) When the figures are arranged, draw an arc across the top edges of the board.

Make small markings on the particleboard with the point of a nail to mark the placements of the wood appliqué motifs. Remove the figures from the board.

Cut the arc on the particleboard and rout the edges; or round the edges with sandpaper if you do not have a router. Prime, then paint, particleboard on all sides. Glue the motifs to the headboard. Overlap the motifs atop the nail head markings.

Bolt the headboard to the frame using bolts, nuts, and washers.

Appliquéd Bed Linens and Dust Ruffle

Shown on pages 40–41.

All linens are for a twin-size bed.

MATERIALS

Purchased sheets, pillowcase, and dust ruffle

For the dust ruffle

½ yard of green cotton fabric for stems and leaves

⅛ yard *each* of lavender, pink, rose, and yellow cottons for flowers

Fusible webbing or paper-backed webbing

Threads to match fabric colors

For the top sheet and pillowcase

⅛ yard *each* of yellow gingham and solid yellow cotton fabrics for chicks and wings

Scraps of golden yellow cotton for beaks

Fusible webbing or paper backed webbing

Black embroidery floss

Threads to match fabric colors

INSTRUCTIONS

PREPARING THE PATTERNS: Trace the full-size patterns (flowers on page 47 and chick on page 50) onto tracing paper. Cut out

shapes. Then cut out the parts of each motif to make the appliqué patterns. The heavy lines around the motifs indicate the pattern shapes. Make cardboard templates for each pattern.

CUTTING THE PIECES: *Note:* If you use paper-backed fusible webbing for appliqué assembly, press this webbing to appliqué fabrics *before you draw and cut out the pieces.*

For the dust ruffle, draw the patterns atop the *right* sides of fabrics as follows: Draw 8 lavender and 8 yellow tulips, 6 rose and 6 pink roses, 16 green tulip stems and leaves, and 12 green rose stems and leaves. Draw the details of the flowers and leaves atop the fabric pieces.

For the top sheet and pillowcase, draw and cut out 17 chick bodies from the solid yellow fabric, 17 wings from yellow gingham fabric, and 17 beaks from golden yellow fabric.

Cut matching shapes for all pieces from fusible webbing if you are not using paper-backed fusible webbing.

ASSEMBLY: For the dust ruffle, beginning at the top left side edge of the ruffle, fuse the *center* of one tulip stem 7½ inches from the side edge and 2½ inches from the hem. Working around the skirt, alternate the tulip and rose stems, placing the stems 13½

inches apart and 2½ inches from the skirt hem.

When all stems are in place, fuse the flowers atop the stems in the following color and flower sequence, beginning from the left side edge: a lavender tulip, a pink rose, a yellow tulip, and a rose-colored rose. Then machine-zig-zag around the shapes and their details using matching threads.

For the sheet, fold the sheet in half, *lengthwise,* and mark the center. Referring to the diagram, *above,* fuse two chick bodies (one to the left and one to the right of the center mark), having the lower edges of their bodies 2¼ inches from the hem edge. Referring to the diagram, *above,* fuse three chick bodies to the right of this grouping, all facing toward the center. The first of these chicks is 3¾ inches from the tail end of the center chick. Then fuse the two-chick grouping to the right of this grouping. The first of these chicks is 5 inches from the tail end of the third chick.

Follow the above sequence for fusing the chicks to the left of the center left chick.

Fuse wings and beaks in place.

Machine-zigzag around all the shapes with matching threads. Draw legs and feet and zigzag atop these lines. Atop each chick, satin-stitch one black eye, using two threads of embroidery floss.

For the pillowcase, rip out the two seams of the case to ease the
continued

appliquéing. Referring to the photograph on page 41, fuse the two-chick grouping along the bottom edge of one corner and the three-chick grouping to the upper right corner of the case. Then seam the two opened edges.

Appliquéd Pillow Sham

Shown on 40.

Finished sham is 20x25 inches.

MATERIALS
Purchased sham
Scraps of solid green, yellow, lavender, rose, pink, blue, peach cotton fabrics
Scraps of striped and pindot blue cotton fabrics and striped pink cotton fabric
Threads to match fabric colors
Scraps of yellow yarns for hair
Fusible webbing, or paper-backed fusible webbing
Pink and black embroidery floss
Scraps of yellow yarn for hair

INSTRUCTIONS
PREPARING THE PATTERNS: Trace the full-size patterns (flowers and stems on page 47, and dancing boy and girl on pages 48–49) onto tracing paper. Cut out shapes. Then cut out the parts of each motif to make the appliqué patterns. The heavy lines around the shapes indicate the pattern pieces. Make cardboard templates for each pattern.

CUTTING THE PIECES: If you use the paper-backed fusible webbing for appliqué assembly, press this webbing to appliqué fabrics *before you draw and cut out the pieces.*

Draw the patterns atop *right* sides of fabrics as follows: Draw one lavender and one yellow tulip, and two tulip green stems and leaves. Draw stitching details of flowers and leaves atop fabrics.

For girl, from rose, cut skirt and bandanna; from pink, cut feet, cheek, and dress tie; from striped pink, cut sleeve and skirt trim; from peach, cut hand and face.

For boy, from blue, cut pants, sleeve, and hat tassel; from blue stripe, cut shirt bodice; from blue pindot, cut hat and shoes.

Cut matching shapes for all pieces from fusible webbing if you are not using paper-backed fusible webbing.

ASSEMBLY: For ease in assembly, rip out three sides of the sham. Center the dancing girl and boy atop the sham. Referring to the photograph on page 40 for placement, lay the motifs atop the fabric and fuse in place. Place snippets of yellow yarn under the head pieces before fusing these pieces to the sham. Then machine-zigzag-stitch around the shapes and their details with matching threads. Outline the mouths with pink embroidery floss. Use black floss to satin-stitch the eyes and long stitches for eyelashes.

Reseam the sham edges.

Airplane Quilt

Shown on pages 42–43.

Finished quilt is approximately 64½x79½ inches.

MATERIALS
3½ yards of white cotton fabric
2 yards of bright blue cotton fabric
3 yards of medium blue cotton fabric
5 yards of backing fabric
Quilt batting

INSTRUCTIONS
The quilt is made of 32 airplane blocks and 31 plain blocks, *each* 7½ inches square when assembled into the quilt. The blocks are sewn into nine rows; *each* row has seven blocks.

Use ¼-inch seam allowances throughout. Sew all pieces together with right sides facing.

PREPARING THE PATTERNS: Referring to the drawing of the partial airplane block, *right,* trace and make full-size patterns for the A, C, D, F, and G pieces. Make

cardboard templates for all patterns A through H.

CUTTING THE PIECES: Trace around the templates onto the wrong side of the fabric. Cut out shapes, adding ¼-inch seam allowances to all sides. All cutting directions for the strips and the 8-inch blocks include ¼-inch seam allowances.

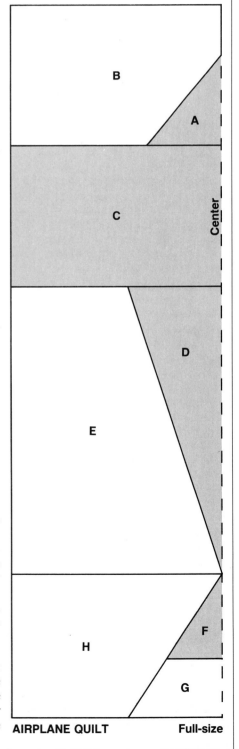

AIRPLANE QUILT   **Full-size**

From the bright blue fabric, cut six strips, *each* measuring 2x44-inches. Cut 32 *each* of templates A, C, D, and F.

From white fabric, cut three strips, *each* 5x44 inches, and six strips, *each* 3x44 inches. Cut 32 *each* of G, B, E, and H. Turn template over and cut 32 *each* of the mirror-images of B, E, and H.

From medium blue fabric, cut two strips, *each* 6½x65 inches, and two strips, *each* 6½x68 inches for borders. Cut 31 blocks, *each* 8 inches square.

TO ASSEMBLE THE BLOCKS: Piece 32 airplanes blocks, referring to the diagram, *right*. The B, E, and H pieces are paired with the corresponding mirror images within the blocks.

To make sashing strips for the blocks, sew a bright blue 2x44-inch strip to *each* long side of the white 5x44-inch strips. Press the seams toward the blue strips.

On the wrong side of one pieced strip, draw parallel lines every 2 inches to divide the strip into 2x8-inch sections. Stack and pin the three strips together with the marked strip on top; cut on the drawn lines through all layers.

Sew one 2x8-inch sashing strip to opposite sides of the 32 pieced airplanes blocks. All blocks are now 8 inches square.

ASSEMBLY OF QUILT TOP: The airplane blocks are alternated with plain blocks to make the nine rows. Make rows 1, 3, 5, 7, and 9 from four pieced blocks and three plain blocks; make rows 2, 4, 6, and 8 from four plain blocks and three pieced blocks. Sew the nine rows together in sequence.

Sew one 6½x68-inch medium blue border strip to *each* long side of the pieced top. Sew one 6½x65-inch medium blue border strip to *each* short side of the quilt top.

FINISHING: Layer the top, batting, and backing; baste together. Cut away the excess batting and backing to within 2 inches of the quilt top. Outline-quilt the airplane block. Quilt the border and plain blocks as desired. Cut away the excess batting and backing.

For the binding, sew the white 3x44-inch strips into one long strip. Fold the binding strip in half, *lengthwise,* wrong sides together. Sew the binding to quilt top, right sides facing. Turn binding to back side; stitch in place.

Pillow Sham

Shown on page 43.

Finished size is 20x35½ inches.

MATERIALS
1½ yards of blue cotton fabric
½ yard of white cotton fabric
⅜ yard of red cotton fabric
2¼ yards of ⅛-inch-diameter cotton cording
3½ yards of ⅜-inch-diameter cotton cording
¼ yard of fusible webbing
21x37-inch piece of fleece

INSTRUCTIONS
Note: All cutting measurements include ¼-inch seam allowances.

PREPARING THE PATTERNS: The airplane for the quilt on page 52 is used for the appliqué pattern. Trace, then transfer to cardboard, the outline of the plane. Make a separate pattern for the tail piece. Draw, then transfer to cardboard, a 2¾-inch square.

CUTTING THE PIECES: From blue fabric, cut two rectangles, *each* 20½x26½-inches for pillow back. Cut 48 squares and one airplane and one tail.

From the white fabric, cut 48 squares; for center panel, cut one 7½x36-inch rectangle

From red fabric, cut two 1x38-inch strips for narrow piping. Cut three 1½x44-inch strips for the wide piping. Cut three airplanes and tails. From the fusible webbing, cut four airplanes and tails.

ASSEMBLY OF SHAM TOP: Sew the top panel in a checkerboard of blue and white squares. Sew 16 squares (8 blue, 8 white) together to make one row. Make four rows, beginning each row with alternating color squares.

Sew rows together for top panel.

Make two more rows; sew the rows together to complete bottom panel. Press seams.

Lay the white panel in a horizontal position. Fold the panel in half, *lengthwise;* then fold in half again, and press lightly atop the folds. Unfold the strip. Position an airplane in each quarter, placing the blue airplane in the third quarter. Fuse the airplanes in place. Machine-appliqué around the airplane, adding stitching to define the wing shape.

Cut the narrow cording in half. Cover each piece with the 1x38-inch red piping strips. Baste piping to the long edges of the white panel. Sew top and bottom panels to the white panel. Cut fleece to match top; baste to wrong side.

FINISHING: Sew the 1½-inch red strips together to make one long length. Cover wide cording. Sew cording to all sides of sham.

Press under 1 inch, then 1 inch again, on *one* short side of *each* blue rectangle; machine-hem. Pin the rectangles to the sham top, *right* sides facing. Overlap the hemmed edges at the center. Sew front and back together. Clip the corners; turn right side out.

Cross-Stitched Shutter Inserts

Shown on page 42.

Each insert is 5x24¼ inches.

MATERIALS
Four pieces of 11-count white Aida cloth, *each* 9x28 inches
DMC embroidery floss: 6 skeins of light blue (No. 799), 4 skeins of dark blue (No. 797), and 2 skeins of red (No. 321)
Purchased shutters with a 5x24¼-inch insert opening
Four tempered hardboard panels, *each* 5x24¼ inches
Four pieces of polyester fleece, *each* 5x24¼ inches
Four pieces of white cotton fabric, *each* 6x25¼ inches
Staple gun

continued

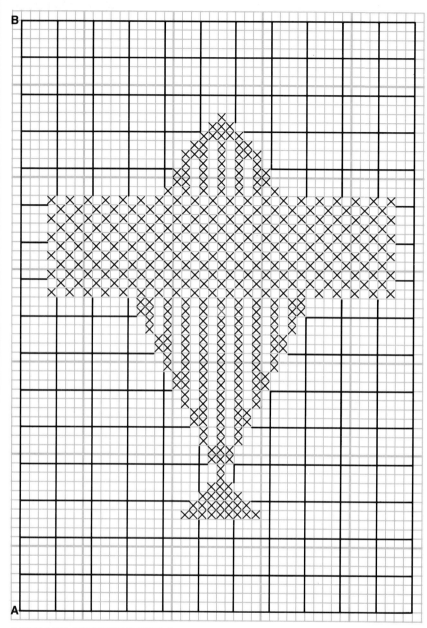

AIRPLANE SHUTTER PANELS   1 Square = 1 Stitch

INSTRUCTIONS

With red floss, stitch the center plane on the two *center* panels and the top plane on the two *outside* panels. Remaining planes are stitched with dark blue floss. Work the grid in backstitches with light blue floss.

To make one shutter insert, refer to the chart, *above*. Locate the center of the Aida cloth and the center of the motif (at the red X); begin stitching there. Work cross-stitches with three strands of the floss over one fabric thread. Work backstitches for the grid over four fabric threads.

Work the complete design from A to B. Then repeat the complete design (from A to B) *above* and *below* the center design. There will be four grids between each of the airplane motifs. Work three additional rows of grid squares at the top and bottom of the panel.

When the stitching is complete, use a warm iron to press the piece on the wrong side.

Lay one strip of fleece atop the hardboard panel. Center cross-stitched strip atop fleece, taking the raw edges to the back side and staple in place.

To finish the back side of the shutter insert, press under ½ inch on the raw edges of white fabric strip. Hand-sew the fabric to the Aida cloth on back of insert.

Fit the covered insert into the shutter opening and tack in place with brads or glazing points.

Repeat the *above* instructions to make three remaining inserts.

Airplane Pillows

Shown on pages 44–45.

Finished striped pillow is 15x20 inches. Finished checked pillow is 14x14 inches.

MATERIALS
For the striped pillow
¾ yard of blue cotton fabric
¼ yard of white cotton fabric
¼ yard of red cotton fabric
2⅛ yards of ⅜-inch-diameter cotton cording
15x20-inch piece of fleece
¼ yard of fusible webbing
Polyester fiberfill
For the checked pillow
½ yard of red cotton fabric
¼ yard *each* of blue and white cotton fabrics
1⅔ yards of ⅜-inch-diameter cotton cording
14-inch square of fleece
¼ yard of fusible webbing
Polyester fiberfill

INSTRUCTIONS
Note: All cutting measurements include ¼-inch seam allowances.

PREPARING THE PATTERNS: The airplane on page 52 is the appliqué pattern for the checked pillow. Make cardboard templates for the airplane and tail pieces.

To make the appliqué pattern for the striped pillow, use a photocopier to make a 50% enlargement of the airplane. Trace, then transfer to cardboard the airplane and tail pieces.

Draw a 2¾-inch square onto graph paper. Trace, then transfer to cardboard to make a template.

To make the striped pillow

CUTTING THE PIECES: From the blue fabric, cut five strips, *each* 2¾x22-inches. Cut one 15x20-inch rectangle for the pillow back.

From the white fabric, cut six strips, *each* 2¾x22-inches.

From red fabric, cut two strips, *each* 1½x44-inches, to cover the cording for piping. Cut 3 tails and 3 airplanes.

From the fusible webbing, cut 3 airplanes and 3 tails.

ASSEMBLY: Sew the blue and white strips together, alternating colors. Press seams toward blue fabric strips.

Place the pillow back *diagonally* atop the pieced strips. Use the pillow back as a pattern to cut the pillow front.

Center one airplane atop the pillow front, 2½ inches from the top edge; position an airplane to each side, 2½ inches from bottom edge. Fuse the airplanes in place. Machine-appliqué around all the shapes, adding stitching across the planes to define the wings. Baste fleece to the wrong side of the pillow top.

FINISHING: Sew the red strips together to make one long strip; cover the cording. Baste the piping to pillow top, right sides together, using ¼-inch seams. Sew pillow back to pillow front, right sides together; leave opening for turning. Clip the corners, turn, and stuff. Sew the opening closed.

To make the checked pillow

CUTTING THE PIECES: Use the enlarged airplane template to cut 1 large airplane and tail section from blue fabric. For piping, cut 2 strips, *each* 1½x30 inches.

From the red fabric, cut a 14-inch square for the pillow back.

Use the 2¾-inch-square template to mark and cut 18 squares.

From the white fabric, mark and cut 18 squares, using the 2¾-inch-square template.

Cut the airplane shapes from the fusible webbing.

ASSEMBLY OF PILLOW TOP: Sew the top in a checkerboard of red and white squares. Sew 6 squares (3 red, 3 white) together to make one row. Make 6 rows. (Begin each successive row with alternating color squares to achieve the checkerboard.) Sew rows together to complete the top.

Center the airplane diagonally on the pieced top with the nose and tail about 5 inches from the corners. Fuse in place. Machine-appliqué around the airplane and tail, adding stitching to define the wings. Baste fleece to the wrong side of the pillow top.

FINISHING: Sew the blue strips together to make a long strip; cover the cording. Baste the piping to pillow top, right sides together, using ¼-inch seams.

Sew the pillow back to the pillow front, right sides together; leave opening for turning. Clip corners, turn, and stuff. Sew the opening closed.

Stenciled Bulletin Board

Shown on page 45.

The finished bulletin board frame is 30½x31½ inches.

MATERIALS
9 feet of 1x6-inch pine board
21x22-inch piece of fiberboard for bulletin board
Five 2½-inch Shaker pegs
⅜-inch-diameter wood dowel
Drill, ½-inch and ⅜-inch bits
Router, ½x⅜-inch bit
Carpenter's glue; wood primer
Twelve ¾x17 brads
Blue latex paint
White stencil paint
1 sheet of acetate or other stenciling material
Stencil brush
Permanent fine-tip marker
Paper towels; drafting tape
Utility knife; picture wire

INSTRUCTIONS

BUILDING THE FRAME: Trim the 1x6-inch board to 5 inches wide. For the frame top and bottom pieces, cut two boards, *each* 31½ inches long; for the frame sides, cut two boards, *each* 20½ inches long.

Butt-joint the frame parts using 1-inch-long dowels and glue. Assemble the frame with two dowels in each joint.

Cut a ½x⅜-inch rabbet on back of center frame with a router.

Prime the frame and Shaker pegs; paint with blue paint.

STENCILING: Trim the acetate sheet to measure 6½x7½ inches. Center the acetate sheet atop the airplane pattern, page 52, with the length of the plane running along the 7½-inch edge. Trace the airplane outline using a permanent marker. Tape the acetate sheet onto a cut-proof work surface. Holding the utility knife like a pencil, cut out the stencil.

Stenciling is done with a dry brush. Dip the tip of the stencil brush into a small amount of stencil paint. Hold the brush upright and work it in a circular motion on a paper towel, removing excess paint and working paint into the bristles.

Using a circular brush motion, work from the stencil-cut edge gradually toward the design center. Repeat the brushing process to achieve greater color intensity. Carefully remove the stencil.

Place the stencil pattern atop the top left side of the frame, referring to the photo on page 45 for plane direction; tape in place. Mark the right edge of the stencil pattern on the frame with a light pencil line. The cut stencil includes the spacing between the airplanes.

To stencil the next airplane to the right, simply place the left edge of the stencil atop the drawn line and tape in place.

Repeat the instructions, *above,* to stencil the two planes on the top right side of the frame but place the right edge of the stencil atop the drawn line.

To stencil the planes on the side edges of the frame, place the stencil 4½ inches from the bottom edge with the nose pointing

continued

toward the top of the frame. Move the stencil as directed on page 55 to complete the next two planes on each side.

FINISHING: Mark the positions for Shaker pegs 2½ inches from the bottom frame edge. Mark the center peg 15¼ inches from the frame sides; mark the two outside pegs 2½ inches from the frame sides. Center and mark the remaining two pegs between the center and outside pegs.

Use a ½-inch drill bit to drill ⅝-inch-deep holes atop the markings. Glue pegs in holes.

Fit the bulletin board into the frame opening; fasten at an angle with brads. Attach picture wire to hang the board.

Soft Sculptured Toy Airplane

Shown on page 44.

Finished airplane is 10½ inches long.

MATERIALS
¼ yard of royal blue fabric
⅛ yard *each* of medium blue, white, and red fabrics
⅔ yard of ½-inch-wide red grosgrain ribbon
Two ½-inch-diameter white buttons
1 large snap
Red and white felt scraps
½-inch-diameter red pompon
Two 1-inch-diameter screen door rollers
⅜-inch-diameter dowel, 3 inches long
Red acrylic paint
Fabric glue
Polyester fiberfill

INSTRUCTIONS
Note: Use ¼-inch seam allowances; do not add seam allowances to felt pieces. Sew all seams with right sides facing.

Trace and make patterns from cardboard for the full-size airplane patterns, *opposite*.

BODY: Trace one airplane body onto the *wrong* side, in the upper half, of the royal blue fabric. Fold the lower half of the fabric under the drawn plane, *right* sides together. Sew atop the drawn line, through both thicknesses; leave the bottom and top edges open between the dots. Cut out body, leaving ¼-inch seams.

Adding ¼-inch seams, cut gusset from the royal blue fabric. With *right* sides facing, pin, then sew, the gusset to the bottom of the plane, matching dots.

Clip curves; turn plane right side out and stuff. Sew the top opening closed.

Cut two windows from white felt and two window trim pieces from red felt. Glue to *each* side of airplane body, referring to the body pattern for placement.

Cut two body trim strips, *each* ½x6½ inches, from the white felt. Glue a felt strip to *each* side of the body, using the shaded area on the pattern as a guide.

Sew buttons at the X on *each* side of the tail. From the red felt, cut two 1¼-inch-diameter circles. Pink or scallop the edge of the circles. Cut a ½-inch-long slit for a buttonhole in the center of *each* circle; slip circles over buttons.

TAIL WINGS: Cut two strips from white felt, *each* ⅜x4½ inches. Trace two tail wings onto the *wrong* side, in the upper half, of the medium blue fabric. Fold the lower half of the fabric under the drawn tails, *right* sides together. Then sew atop the drawn lines, through both thicknesses, leaving openings between dots.

Cut out wings, adding ¼-inch seam allowances. Clip the curves, turn right side out, and stuff. Sew the openings closed. Glue two felt strips around the tail wing, using the shaded area on the pattern as a guide. Sew the tail wings to airplane, using the dashed lines on the plane body pattern as a guide.

PROPELLER: Trace one propeller onto the *wrong* side, in the upper half, of the medium blue fabric. Fold the lower half of the fabric under the drawn propeller, *right* sides together. Sew through both thicknesses atop the drawn line; leave an opening between the dots for turning. Cut out propeller, adding seam allowances. Clip the curves; turn, and stuff. Sew the opening closed.

Sew the flat side of the snap to the nose of the airplane; sew the matching snap piece to the center of one side of the propeller. Snap the propeller onto the airplane. Glue pompon to the center of the propeller.

WHEELS: Paint the dowel red. Glue a screen door roller to each end of the dowel. Cut a ⅝x1½-inch strip from the red felt. Position the wheels under the plane at the front end of the gusset. Loop the felt strip around the dowel; sew the short ends of the strip to the plane to hold the dowel in place.

WING: From the red fabric, cut four strips, *each* 2¼x8 inches. From the white fabric, cut two strips, *each* 1½x8 inches, and one strip 2¼x8 inches.

Sew the strips together to form a rectangle, alternating red and white strips with the wide white strip in center. Press all seams toward the red strips. Fold strip in half, *right* sides together. Trace the wing pattern onto the *wrong* side of the fabric. Sew atop the drawn line, leaving an opening between the dots. Cut out the wing, adding ¼-inch seams. Clip curves; turn right side out, and stuff. Sew the opening closed.

Fold the ribbon in half and finger-press center fold; center and tack the ribbon, *lengthwise,* to the top of plane where the opening was closed. Tack along both sides of the ribbon and 1 inch on both sides of the fold. Use the ribbon to tie the wing to the plane.

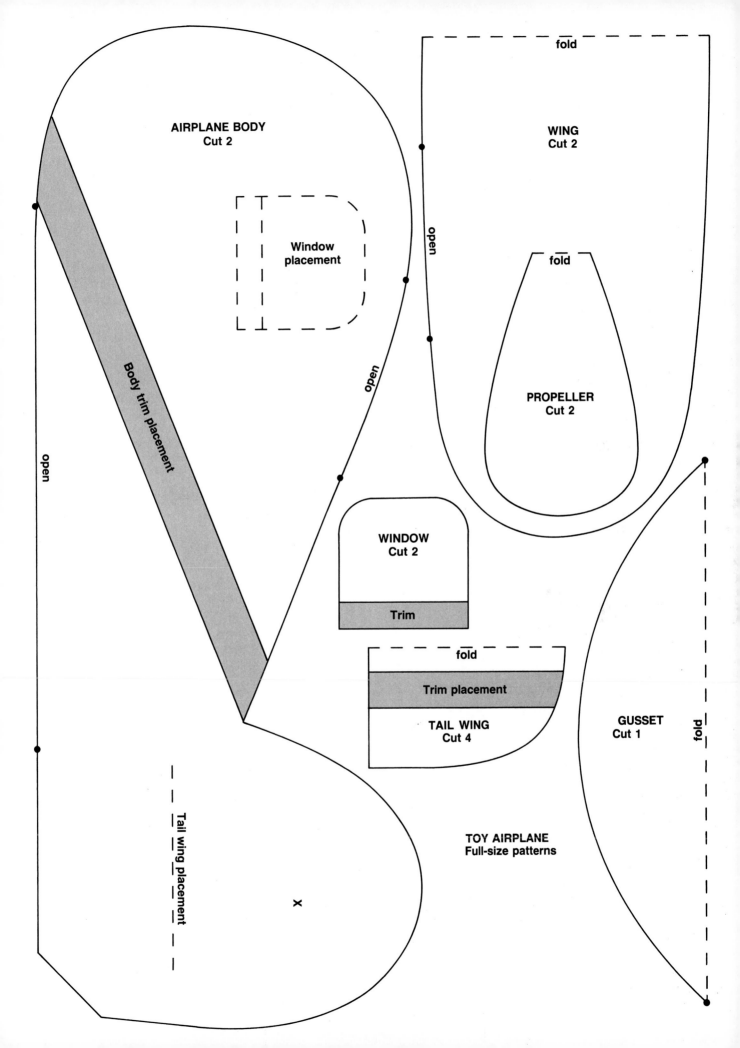

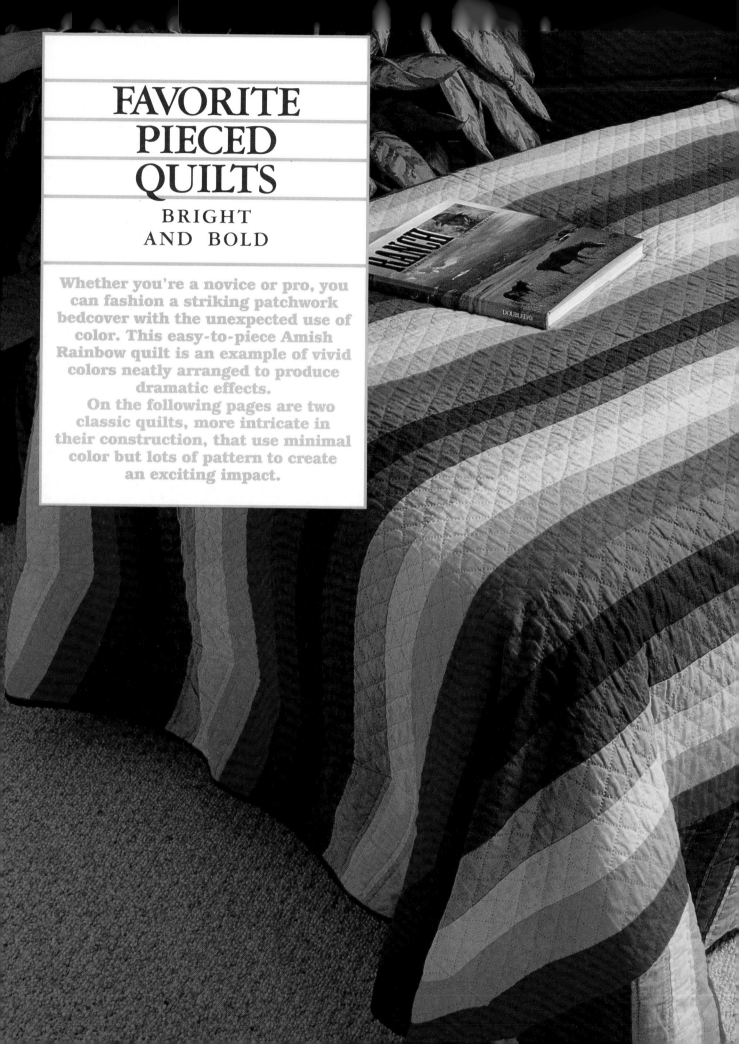

FAVORITE PIECED QUILTS

BRIGHT AND BOLD

Whether you're a novice or pro, you can fashion a striking patchwork bedcover with the unexpected use of color. This easy-to-piece Amish Rainbow quilt is an example of vivid colors neatly arranged to produce dramatic effects.

On the following pages are two classic quilts, more intricate in their construction, that use minimal color but lots of pattern to create an exciting impact.

he Rainbow quilt featured here was designed as a coverlet by the Pennsylvania Amish. Simple, straight lines in the quilting and piecing give this quilt dignity and drama.

Thirty-five red, gold, yellow, green, teal, navy, and purple strips, easily pieced on your sewing machine, form the top of this 86x90-inch spread. Diagonal strips and square blocks in the corners complete the border.

Instructions for the quilts in this section begin on page 62.

A patchwork tour de force, the superb Golden Glow quilt, *above,* is a challenge for an avid quilt maker.

This quilt measures 77x89 inches and is composed of forty-two blocks, each 12 inches square.

When worked in any color but yellow, this pattern is named the Star Dahlia. You also can work this design in assorted colors using your fabric scraps. Choose any of these colorations to create an heirloom bed covering for your home.

The 74-inch-square Delectable Mountains quilt, *opposite,* uses a pattern that dates to the 1800s. Easy to assemble, this traditional quilt is pieced from the center block to its sides.

Amish Rainbow Quilt

Shown on pages 58–59.

Finished size is 86x90 inches.

MATERIALS

2¼ yards *each* of red, gold, yellow, light green, teal, navy, and purple cotton fabrics
5½ yards backing fabric
Quilt batting

INSTRUCTIONS

Note: It is helpful to mark the various groups of fabric strips to identify their use (borders or center strips). All measurements include ¼-inch seam allowances.

CUTTING THE STRIPS: For the center portion of the quilt, cut five 2½x80-inch strips from *each* of the seven fabrics.

For borders, cut three 2⅜x80-inch strips from *each* of the seven fabrics.

For the border corners, cut one 2¾x80-inch strip *each* from teal, gold, red, and yellow fabrics. The remaining navy fabric is used to make the quilt binding.

PIECING THE CENTER TOP: For the center of the quilt, sew the 35 strips together, *lengthwise,* repeating the color sequence as follows: red, gold, yellow, green, teal, navy, and purple. Trim the ends square so the quilt top measures 74½ inches long.

BORDER CORNERS: Draw a right-angle triangle with 9-inch legs onto graph paper. From cardboard, make a template from this

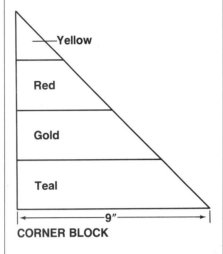

CORNER BLOCK

pattern. From 2¾x80-inch strips of teal, gold, red, and yellow, sew a strip set.

Referring to diagram, *above,* mark and cut 4 triangles facing right, on the wrong side of the strip set, placing the base leg even with the edge of the teal strip. Then flip the template over; mark and cut four more triangles (mirror images of the first four). Pair each triangle with its mirror image; sew to form 4 squares.

PIECING THE BORDERS: For the borders, sew 3 sets of 2⅜x80-inch strips in the same color sequence as the center. Lay one strip set *wrong* side up with the purple edge at the top; square off the left side (the short side). Referring to the diagram, *below,* measure 6 inches from the top left side and mark an X; mark a Y at the lower left corner. Draw a diagonal line from the X to the Y.

To divide this strip set into 8 units, measure 8¾ inches from the X and Y markings and draw a second diagonal line. Continue to measure and draw 8¾-inch parallel lines in this manner to mark 8 units.

Pin the *unmarked* strip sets, *wrong sides up,* underneath the marked set; cut on drawn lines to make 24 border units.

Make four borders by sewing together 6 border units. Matching border colors with center stripes, sew borders to *top* and *bottom* of the quilt. Trim off excess borders along the side edges.

For the side borders, square off remaining two borders to measure 74½ inches. Sew a corner square to *each* end of borders. Sew borders to quilt sides.

FINISHING: Layer the quilt top, batting, and backing. Quilt the center portion in a diagonal grid of 1-inch squares; outline-quilt ¼-inch from seams on the border strips. Round off quilt corners; trim away the excess batting and backing fabric.

To make bias binding, cut 1½-inch-wide strips of navy fabric. Piece strips together; bind edges.

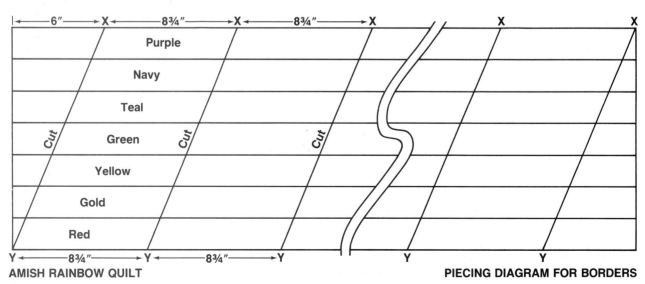

AMISH RAINBOW QUILT **PIECING DIAGRAM FOR BORDERS**

Golden Glow Quilt

Shown on page 60.

Finished size of quilt is approximately 77x89 inches.

MATERIALS
4½ yards of white cotton fabric
5½ yards of yellow cotton fabric
for patchwork and binding
5½ yards of backing fabric
Quilt batting
Water-erasable pen

INSTRUCTIONS
This quilt pattern is known as Golden Glow when it is pieced from yellow and white fabrics. When other color combinations are used, the pattern is generally known as Star Dahlia.

The quilt shown is made of 42 blocks; *each* block is 12 inches square. The blocks are arranged in 7 rows of 6 blocks each.

Note: The border cutting measurements include ¼-inch seam allowances. Add ¼-inch seam allowances to all other pieces.

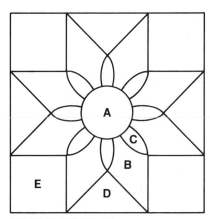

PIECING DIAGRAM

PREPARING THE PATTERNS: From full-size patterns, *right,* make the cardboard templates for A, B, and C. Copy the heavy line placement markings onto template A. (These markings are the gathering guide lines for the C pieces.) To make patterns for D and E, draw a 3½-inch square onto graph paper; draw a diagonal line, dividing the square into two triangles. Template E is the 3½-inch square; template D is the triangle. *continued*

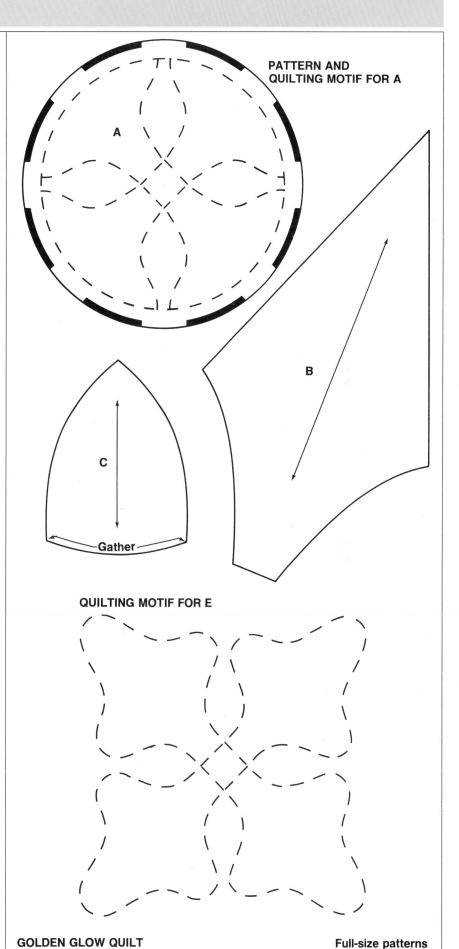

PATTERN AND QUILTING MOTIF FOR A

QUILTING MOTIF FOR E

GOLDEN GLOW QUILT   **Full-size patterns**

CUTTING THE PIECES: From the yellow fabric, cut 2 borders *each* 3x90½ inches and 2 borders *each* 3x72½ inches. For the binding, cut eight 3x44-inch strips. Cut 336 of B and 42 of A. With a water-erasable pen, mark the gathering placement guides on all A circles.

From the white fabric, cut 336 of C, and 168 *each* of D and E. Cut the D triangles with the long side on the straight fabric grain.

ASSEMBLY OF QUILT TOP: Referring to the piecing diagram on page 63, sew 8 B and 8 C pieces together to make a star with an open center. Piece 4 E and 4 D pieces into outer star edges to make a square. Sew a gathering thread atop *each* C piece on the center seam line.

Run a gathering thread around the A piece, ⅛ inch beyond the seam line.

From oaktag or similar weight cardboard, cut a finished-size A circle. Place this circle on the wrong side of the fabric circle; draw up and tie the gathering thread, taking the seam allowance to the wrong side. Press; remove the oaktag circle. Appliqué the circle atop the center opening, pulling up the gathering threads on the C pieces to align with the placement markings on piece A.

Make 42 blocks. Sew the blocks into 7 rows, *each* with 6 blocks; join the rows. Sew the 3x72½-inch borders to the top and bottom of the quilt; center and sew the 3x90½-inch borders to sides.

FINISHING: Layer the top, batting, and backing; baste together. Cut away the excess backing and batting materials to within 2 inches of the quilt top.

Refer to the diagrams on page 63 for the quilt motifs on the E and A pieces. Outline-quilt ¼ inch from the seams on the A, B, and D pieces. The borders are quilted with diagonal parallel lines spaced 1 inch apart.

Cut the batting and backing even with the quilt top; round off quilt corners. Sew the short ends of the binding strips together. Fold the binding in half, having raw edges even. Sew the binding to the quilt top, right sides facing and raw edges even. Turn the binding to the wrong side; hand-stitch in place.

Delectable Mountains Quilt

Shown on page 61.

Finished quilt is approximately 74 inches square.

MATERIALS
3 yards of red cotton fabric
3½ yards of white cotton fabric
¾ yard of red cotton fabric for binding
4¾ yards of backing fabric
Quilt batting

INSTRUCTIONS
Note: Add ¼-inch seam allowances to all pieces. Press seams toward red fabric, when possible, so the red seams do not show on white pieces.

PREPARING THE PATTERNS: Draw the following shapes onto graph paper: For template A, draw a 9-inch square. Divide this square in half *diagonally* to create the triangle for template C. Divide triangle C in half for template B. Template E is a right-angle triangle with 12-inch legs. Make cardboard templates from each of these shapes.

Trace and transfer to cardboard the full-size patterns for templates D and F on page 65.

CUTTING THE PIECES: The E triangles are cut with the *long* side on the straight of the fabric grain; all other triangles are cut with the legs on the straight of the fabric grain.

From the red fabric, cut pieces as follows: 1 of A, 24 of C, 168 of D, and 104 of F.

From the white fabric, cut 16 of E, 20 of C, 4 of B, 168 of D, and 104 of F.

ASSEMBLY OF QUILT TOP: Sew a B triangle to each side of A. Add a red C to each of the four sides to complete center square.

Sew the remaining white C triangles and red C triangles together, along the long sides, to form 20 squares. Piece 8 pairs of C squares along the white sides to make 8 rectangles. (Four red-and-white squares remain.)

Sew pairs of E triangles into 4 large triangles for corners.

Sew red D triangles and white D triangles together to form squares.

Refer to the piecing diagram, *right,* to assemble the diagonal rows. Sew the rows together, repeating rows 2, 3, and 4 on the opposite side of Row 1 to complete the top.

BORDERS: Sew pairs of red and white F triangles together to make squares. Make two borders, *each* with 25 squares; sew these borders to opposite sides of the quilt top. Make two borders, *each* with 27 squares; sew these borders to remaining sides of quilt.

FINISHING: Layer the top, batting, and backing; baste together. Cut away the excess backing and batting materials to within 2 inches of the quilt top. Quilt as desired. Suggested quilting is to outline-quilt all D and F triangles. Quilt parallel lines or a fancy quilting pattern in each of the larger triangles.

Cut the batting and backing even with the quilt top.

From the binding fabric, cut eight 3x44-inch strips; sew the short ends of the strips together. Fold the binding wrong sides together, having raw edges even. Sew the binding to the quilt top, right sides facing and raw edges even. Turn the binding to the wrong side; hand-stitch in place.

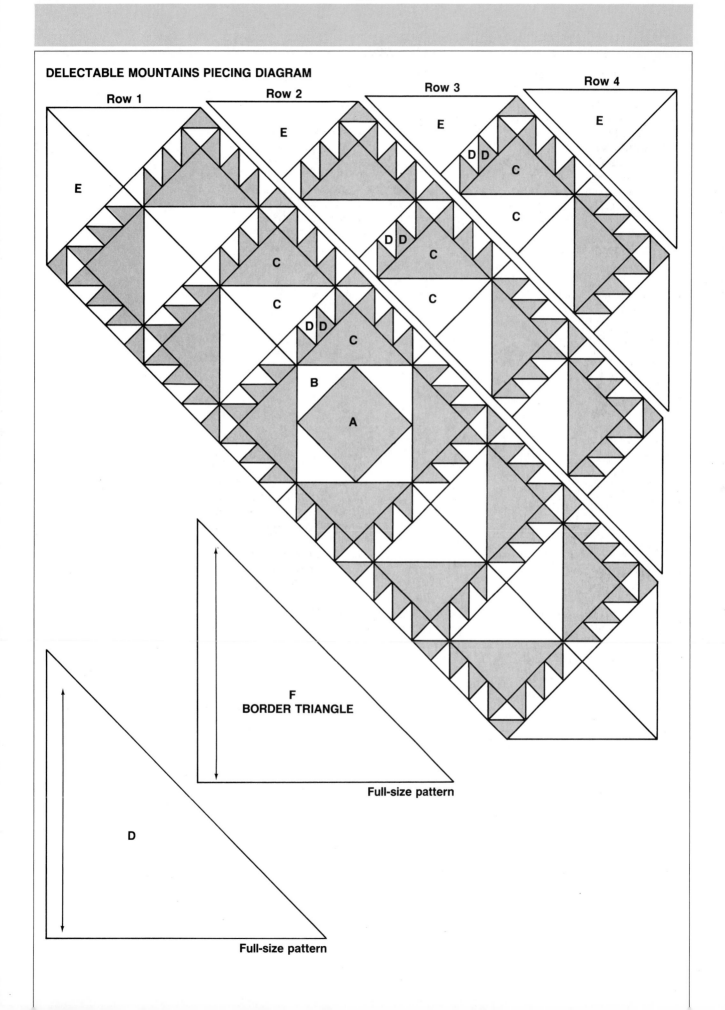

DELECTABLE MOUNTAINS PIECING DIAGRAM

Row 1

Row 2

Row 3

Row 4

E

E

E

E

E

D D

C

C

C

D D

C

C

C

D D

C

B

A

F
BORDER TRIANGLE

Full-size pattern

D

Full-size pattern

HEARTFELT DESIGNS

FOR A MERRY CHRISTMAS

Enjoy an old-time Christmas celebration with homespun surroundings like the ones pictured here. Crisp starched muslin, appliquéd with red and green plaid hearts, brings a special warmth and welcome to your holiday entertaining. More ideas, using these humble materials, are on the next four pages.

The 16x64-inch table runner, *far right,* provides a festive Christmas setting for home-baked cookies, fruits, pastries, and hot apple cider.

Twelve hearts, made from scraps of red and green drapery plaids, are centered and appliquéd to a grid of three-inch squares on both ends of the runner. Plaid bias piping and lots of ruffles add a country-fresh look.

To set yourself off as the hostess of your holiday gatherings, make the apron, *right,* with its heart-covered bib and ruffled skirt.

Plaid pipings outline the apron details; the pockets and ruffled bib trims are optional. Make your apron as plain or as fancy as you like.

Instructions for all of the seasonal projects in this chapter begin on page 72.

Make a favorite child merry with the handcrafted pigtailed doll, *opposite*.

This adorable 18-inch-tall playmate is decked in buttoned shoes, calico dress, and her own hostess apron.

Use simple hand-embroidery stitches for her facial details and brown worsted yarn to fashion her hairdo.

To complete your old-time Christmas decor, stitch the heart tree decorations and skirt, *opposite*.

Twelve red and green appliquéd hearts trim the 51-inch-diameter skirt. Pipings and ruffles define its scalloped edges. To complete the tree skirt embellishments, cut a wide strip from one of the plaids and tie a big bow around the base of the tree.

Use dried baby's-breath with lots of fabric hearts to create this homespun tree.

HEARTFELT DESIGNS

Suspend the oversize stocking, *left,* from the mantel, and it's certain to capture Santa's attention. Then imagine a child's thrill on Christmas morning with all the treasures this stocking can hold.

Stitched from muslin and scraps of plaid fabrics, this sock measures 19 inches tall. Checkered bands, bordered with plaid stripings and three large appliquéd hearts, embellish its front. Plaid bias piping define and outline its shape.

Twenty-five heart pockets on the Advent tree, *above,* are filled with special surprises or treats. Remove one each day during the month of December. When all the pockets are empty, Christmas Day will have arrived.

Each plaid heart is appliquéd to a three-inch-square grid on the muslin base. The plaid piping around the tree adds more stability as it hangs on the wall. A plaid star topper, jingle bells, and satin ribbons complete its yule-time embellishments.

Heart Table Runner

Shown on page 66–67.

Runner is 16x64 inches, including ruffles.

MATERIALS
2 yards of 45-inch-wide muslin
12x60-inch piece of fleece
½ yard of 54-inch-wide red plaid
    fabric for ruffle
Scraps of red-and-green plaid
    fabrics for 24 hearts
4¼ yards of cotton cording
Strip of plaid fabric pieced to
    measure 1½ inches wide and
    4¼ yards for piping
Water-erasable pen

INSTRUCTIONS
Note: ½-inch seam allowances are used throughout unless noted otherwise.

Cut 2 pieces of muslin to measure 13x61 inches. Set one piece aside for backing. Using the water-erasable pen, at *each* end of one muslin piece and inside the seam allowance, draw a 9x12-inch rectangle. Divide rectangle into 3-inch squares (there will be three rows, with four squares in each row).

Center and baste fleece to the unmarked side of muslin. Machine-quilt atop the drawn lines.

Trace heart pattern 2, *right,* onto tissue paper; cut out. Trace 24 hearts onto *wrong* side of assorted plaids; do not cut out. With right sides facing, place muslin scraps behind the heart drawings and stitch around the entire heart shapes. Cut out the hearts, leaving ¼-inch seams; clip curves. Make a small slit in the centers of the muslin; turn the hearts right side out and press.

Hand-appliqué the hearts atop each of the 24 squares.

For the piping, cover the cotton cording with 1½-inch-wide plaid fabric. Stitch piping atop seam line of right side of muslin.

For the ruffle, cut six 3-inch-wide strips the full width of the plaid fabric. Piece strips to measure 9 yards long; sew strip together to form a circle.

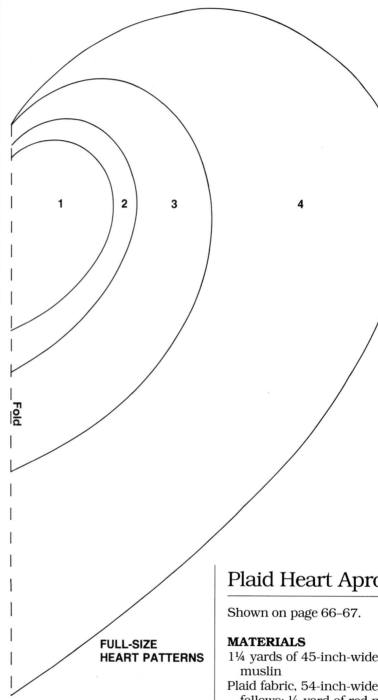

1 **2** **3** **4**

Fold

**FULL-SIZE
HEART PATTERNS**

Press under ¼ inch twice along one long edge; machine stitch for narrow hem.

Stitch two rows of gathering threads along opposite edge of ruffle. Pull up gathers to fit edges of runner. With right sides facing, sew ruffle atop piping seam line.

With right sides facing, sew the backing to the runner top, keeping ruffle free from seam and leaving a 6-inch opening for turning. Clip seams, turn, and press. Sew opening closed.

Plaid Heart Apron

Shown on page 66–67.

MATERIALS
1¼ yards of 45-inch-wide
    muslin
Plaid fabric, 54-inch-wide, as
    follows: ¼ yard of red plaid for
    bib and pocket ruffles and 2
    hearts; ¾ yard of second red
    plaid for neck strap,
    waistband, ties, and 1 heart;
    ⅓ yard of third red plaid for
    top skirt ruffle and two
    hearts; ½ yard of green plaid
    for bottom skirt ruffle, piping,
    and four hearts
10-inch square of fleece
2½ yards of cotton cording for
    piping; water-erasable pen

INSTRUCTIONS

Note: Use ½-inch seam allowances throughout, *except* for the heart appliqués. On these add ¼-inch seam allowances.

From muslin, cut two 10-inch squares for bib and bib lining, one 21x42-inch rectangle for the skirt, four 7¼x8-inch pieces for pockets and pocket linings, and nine pattern 2 hearts, *left.*

From ¼ yard of one red plaid fabric, cut one 3x54-inch strip for bib ruffle, two 2x16-inch strips for pocket ruffles, and two hearts.

From second red plaid, cut one 4x24-inch length on the bias for the neck strap, two 2½x29-inch lengths on the bias for the waistband and waistband facing, four 5x31-inch lengths for the ties, and one heart.

From third red plaid, cut and piece one 5½x84-inch strip for top skirt ruffle and two hearts.

From green plaid, cut one 1¼x28-inch bias strip for bib piping, one 1¼x42-inch bias strip for skirt piping, and two 1¼x8-inch bias strips for the pocket pipings, and four hearts. Cut and piece one 7x84-inch length for bottom skirt ruffle.

APPLIQUÉS: With right sides facing, sew plaid hearts to muslin backings, using ¼-inch seams. Cut slits in centers of muslin; clip curves, turn, and press.

BIB: With water-erasable pen, center and draw a 9-inch square on one of the 10-inch muslin squares. Divide this square into nine 3-inch squares. Baste the fleece to the unmarked side of the square and machine-quilt atop the drawn lines. Hand-appliqué hearts to centers of each square.

Cover the cotton cording with the 28-inch green plaid and sew piping to sides and top of bib.

Press under ¼ inch twice on one long edge and on the two short ends of the 3x54-inch red plaid; hem. Sew two rows of gathering thread on remaining side. Gather ruffle to fit bib top and sides. With right sides facing, sew ruffle atop piping seam.

Fold 4x24-inch red plaid neck strap in half lengthwise. Sew a seam the entire length, leaving ends open for turning. Trim seam allowance to ¼ inch; turn and press. Baste strap ends to wrong side of bib front inside the side seam allowances at sides of bib.

With piping, ruffle, and neck strap facing inward, sew muslin backing to bib front, leaving the bottom edge open. Clip seams, turn, and press. Baste layers together across bottom of bib.

SKIRT: Cover the cording with green plaid pocket bias strips. Sew pipings along top edges of pockets atop seam lines. Hem one long edge of *each* red pocket ruffles; run gathering threads along opposite edges. Gather the ruffles and sew them atop piping seam lines, tapering ends at side edges.

With right sides facing, sew the pocket linings to pockets, leaving an opening for turning. Turn and press. Position pockets on skirt 3½ inches down from waistline and 5 inches from the center front. Topstitch pockets in place.

Turn under ½ inch twice on sides of apron; hem. Cover the cording with bias green piping strip; sew piping to skirt hem.

Hem one long side and two short sides of both skirt ruffles. Gather remaining long edges to fit bottom of skirt. Sew narrow red ruffle atop the wide green ruffle. With right sides facing, sew ruffles atop piping seam line.

With right sides facing, fold one red tie end in half *lengthwise* and sew together the long side and *one* short end. Trim seams to ¼ inch; turn, and press. Make a tuck in the unstitched end to fit short end of waistband, leaving the seam allowances free. Stitch in place. Repeat instructions for other tie.

Gather top edge of skirt to measure 22 inches; sew this edge to waistband, right sides facing and matching center front.

Pin the waistband facing to top edge of waistband, centering bib in between (face bib downward, atop skirt) and keeping tie ends free. Sew through all thicknesses across skirt; clip seams, turn. Press under facing raw edge and slip-stitch in place.

Heart Tree Skirt

Shown on page 68–69.

Tree skirt is 51 inches in diameter, including ruffle.

MATERIALS
3½ yards of 45-inch-wide muslin
1¼ yards of 45-inch-wide fleece
¼ yard *each* of four 54-inch-wide plaid fabrics for heart appliqués
¾ yard of 54-inch-wide plaid fabric for ruffle
Strip of plaid fabric, pieced to measure 1½ inches wide and 5 yards long for piping
5 yards of cotton cording
Tissue paper

INSTRUCTIONS
MAKING THE PATTERN: Tape sheets of tissue paper together to make a 24-inch square. Using a string and pencil, draw a quarter-circle with a radius of 22½ inches. Cut away the paper outside the circle drawing. Fold the pattern into thirds (pattern will be cone-shape). Measure 2½ inches down from the widest sides of the

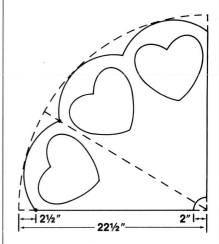

cone and mark the two points with pencil. Draw a line through the center of the cone from the point to the center top. Draw an arc from the 2½-inch markings to the center marking to establish

continued

the scallop edge. Cut away paper beyond the scallop; unfold paper.

At center point of pattern, draw a quarter-circle atop the pattern with a 2-inch radius (tree trunk opening); cut away this portion.

From muslin, cut one 45-inch square. Fold the square in half twice, making it a 22½-inch square. Pin the tissue pattern atop the folded muslin square, having one straight edge atop fold lines. Cut out muslin (do not cut the folded edge). Unfold the fabric.

Cut a straight line from the outside edge of the muslin skirt to the center opening. Begin to cut between any two scallops.

Cut another matching shape from muslin for backing and one from fleece for padding. Set one muslin piece aside. Baste fleece to wrong side of other muslin piece.

Trace heart pattern 4 on page 72 onto tissue paper; cut out. Trace 12 hearts onto wrong side of assorted plaids; do not cut out. Place muslin behind the heart drawings and stitch around the entire heart shapes, right sides facing. Cut out hearts, leaving ¼-inch seams. Cut slit in center of hearts on the muslin sides; clip curves, turn, and press.

Center and hand-appliqué the hearts along the scallop edges. Position hearts 3¼ inches from the outside edge of the skirt.

For the piping, cover the cotton cording with 1½-inch-wide plaid fabric. Stitch piping atop the scalloped edge of skirt.

Cut six 4x54-inch strips of fabric for the ruffle. Sew strips together to make one long length, with the right sides facing. Machine-stitch a narrow hem along one long side of strip, folding fabric under ¼ inch twice. Run two gathering threads along opposite side of strip. Gather fabric to fit scalloped edge; sew in place.

With right sides facing and piping and ruffle facing inward, sew muslin backing to top of skirt. Sew around entire piece, leaving opening for turning. Clip curves and turn. Sew opening closed.

Machine-quilt ¼ inch from the edge of *each* heart. Topstitch along the scalloped edge, straight edges, and the center cutout.

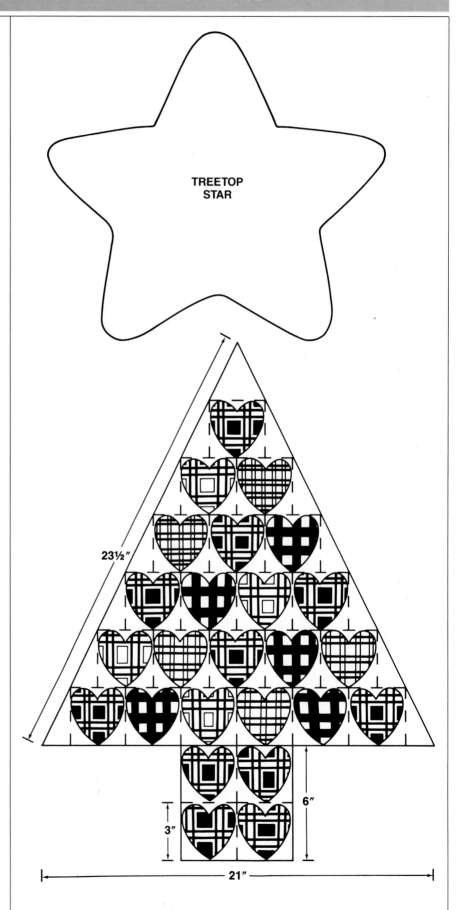

TREETOP STAR

23½"

6"

3"

21"

ADVENT TREE DIAGRAM

Heart Advent Tree

Shown on page 71.

Wall hanging is 27 inches tall.

MATERIALS

1½ yards of 45-inch-wide muslin
25x31-inch piece of fleece
⅛ yard *each* of three red plaid fabrics
¼ yard of green plaid fabric
3-yard length of 1½-inch-wide green plaid fabric for piping
3 yards of cotton cording
¾-inch-diameter plastic ring
14 small jingle bells
3 yards of ¼-inch-wide red satin ribbon; tissue paper
Dressmaker's carbon paper

INSTRUCTIONS

Trace heart pattern 2, on page 72, onto tissue paper; cut out. Trace 11 green hearts and 14 assorted red hearts onto wrong side of plaid fabric; do not cut out. Place muslin scraps behind the heart drawings and stitch atop the drawn lines, around the entire heart shapes. Cut out the hearts, leaving ¼-inch seams; clip curves. Cut a small slit in the centers of the muslin; turn the hearts right side out and press.

Referring to the diagram, *left,* draw the tree outline onto tissue paper; add ½-inch seam allowances to all sides. Draw a grid of 3-inch squares, as shown on the diagram, inside the seam allowances. Using carbon paper, transfer pattern to muslin.

Baste fleece to the unmarked side of the tree. Topstitch through both layers atop the grid lines.

Hand-sew one heart atop each 3-inch square, leaving the top of the heart open to form a pocket.

Including the ½-inch seam allowance, cut out the tree shape. Cut a backing shape from muslin to match.

Cover cording with green plaid strip to make piping. Sew piping atop seam lines to front of tree.

With right sides facing, sew the front to backing, leaving opening for turning. Trim seams, turn, press, and sew opening closed.

For star on top of tree, use pattern on page 74 and follow the heart directions, *left,* to assemble. Sew star to tree. Tack bells and bows to center of hearts, referring to the photo on page 71. Sew ring to tree back for hanger.

Tuck a small goody in each heart pocket. Each day of December, the child will remove one treat. When the treats are gone, Christmas day has arrived.

Heart Stocking

Shown on page 70.

Stocking stands 19 inches tall.

MATERIALS

1 yard of 45-inch-wide muslin
Two 16x20-inch pieces of fleece for batting
2¼ yards of cotton cording
1x80-inch bias-plaid strip for piping
Scraps of red plaids and green plaids for front stocking trim

INSTRUCTIONS

Enlarge the stocking shape, *below,* onto graph paper and mark the dashed line 6½ inches from the top edge; add ½-inch seam allowances. From the muslin, cut three stocking shapes. From fleece, cut 2 stocking shapes. *For front of stocking,* cut one shape below the dashed line, adding ¼-inch seam allowance above the dashed line.

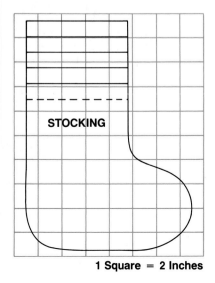

STOCKING

1 Square = 2 Inches

STOCKING FRONT: Using ¼-inch seams, sew a 1¾x10-inch strip of red plaid to top of stocking front. Repeat instructions with a green plaid strip.

To make the two red-and-white checkered strips, cut 7 *each* 1¾-inch squares from muslin and red plaid fabrics. Piece squares, using ¼-inch seams, to make two seven-block strips. One strip has 4 plaid squares and 3 muslin squares; the second has 4 muslin squares and 3 plaid squares. Sew strips together; then sew assembled strip to the top of stocking. Stitch a 2x10-inch strip of green plaid to top of stocking.

Baste one fleece stocking shape to wrong side of stocking front.

Trace heart pattern 3, on page 72, onto tissue paper; add ¼-inch seams. Cut 3 hearts from assorted plaid fabrics and three from muslin for backing. With right sides together, sew hearts to muslin backings; sew around entire hearts. Cut a slit in the muslin hearts; clip curves, turn, and press. Hand-sew hearts in a row on front of stocking foot.

Cover the cording with the red bias-strip. With right sides facing, sew piping to the stocking front atop the ½-inch seam allowance; do not sew piping across top of stocking.

STOCKING BACK: Baste second piece of fleece to one of the full-size muslin stockings for the stocking back. With right sides facing, sew stocking front to stocking back atop piping seams. Sew piping around top of stocking, using ½-inch seams.

For sock hanger, cut a 1½x5-inch-long red plaid strip. Fold under ¼ inch on both long edges. Then fold strip in half with folded edges even; sew folded edges together. Fold the 5-inch strip in half, with raw edges even, and sew hanger to left side of stocking atop the piping seam line. Press seams to inside of the stocking.

LINING: Sew remaining two muslin stockings together; trim seams. Slip lining inside stocking. Fold back seam allowance at top of lining; whipstitch in place.

Holiday Rag Doll

Shown on page 69.

Doll stands 18 inches tall.

MATERIALS
¾ yard of 45-inch-wide muslin
Scraps of red, brown, green, and white embroidery floss
Scraps of brown corduroy and 2 tiny buttons for shoes
6 inches of ¼-inch-wide double-fold brown bias tape for shoe straps; 1 ball of worsted-weight brown yarn for hair
½ yard of print fabric for dress and pantaloon
1¼ yards of ¾-inch-wide ungathered ecru lace with eyelets for ribbon weaving
1¾ yards of ⅛-inch-wide ribbon to weave through lace eyelets and hair ribbons
1 yard of ¼-inch-wide elastic
1x18-inch bias strip of plaid fabric for apron skirt trim
Scrap of plaid fabric for heart appliqué on apron
3 snaps; powdered rouge
Polyester fiberfill
Water-erasable pen
Dressmaker's carbon paper

INSTRUCTIONS
Trace the full-size patterns on pages 77–79 onto tissue paper. All patterns include ¼-inch seam allowances, *except the bottom neck edge on the body,* which includes ⅜-inch seams. Stitch all pieces together with right sides facing unless otherwise noted.

For the doll
Pin pattern body (head, legs, arms, and body) pieces to muslin. Cut out all pieces *except the front head.* Trace around this piece with a water-erasable pen.

FACE: Using dressmaker's carbon paper, transfer facial features to front head. Using two strands of floss, stitch as follows: satin-stitch a red mouth and green eyes; outline-stitch around eyelids with brown; straight-stitch brown eyelashes and nose; and work white French knots for eye highlights. Cut out piece.

BODY: Sew the body and head darts. Stitch body pieces together, leaving the neck edge open. Clip curves, turn, and baste neck edge under ⅜ inch. Stuff firmly with fiberfill.
Sew head pieces together, leaving neck edge open. Clip curves, turn, and stuff. Insert head neck into body and slip-stitch in place.

ARMS: Sew arms together in pairs, leaving openings for turning. Clip curves, turn, and stuff. Sew arms to doll along shoulders.

LEGS/SHOES: Cut shoe pieces from corduroy. Stay-stitch along top edges. Press under ¼ inch along top edge, clipping curves as necessary. Topstitch pressed edge of shoes atop feet (the leg piece). Baste together raw edges of shoe and foot.
Sew legs together in pairs, leaving openings for turning. Clip curves, turn, and stuff. Sew legs to bottom of body.
Topstitch the double-fold bias tape. Cut in half and hand-stitch across shoes for straps, turning under raw edges. Sew buttons to outside of each shoe.

HAIR: Cut a 1x6-inch strip of muslin. Wrap yarn 80 times around a 10x20-inch piece of stiff cardboard. Carefully slip the yarn from the cardboard. Position and spread center of yarn atop muslin strip and sew together (sewing line is down the center of the muslin strip and forms the part).
Position front of part at the dart on the head; hand-sew hair in place. Cut loops and trim evenly. Sew small bows in place.
For curly bangs, wrap the yarn around your finger 12 times; tie loops together to make a bundle. Make 4 or 5 bundles. Tack bundles to top of forehead.

For the clothing
PANTALOON: Cut the pantaloon from print fabric.
Press under ¼ inch twice on bottom edges (legs); stitch.

Sew center front seams. Press under ¼ inch at waistline. Zig-zag-stitch elastic to wrong side, stretching elastic as you sew to ease in fullness to fit waist.
Stitch center back seam; stitch side and crotch seams. Trim all seams; turn.

DRESS: Cut bodice, sleeves, a 1½x12-inch strip for neck ruffle, and a 10x45-inch rectangle for skirt from the print fabric.
Sew darts on bodice front and back. Sew shouder seams.
Press under ½ inch along bottom edges of the sleeves. Zigzag-stitch elastic ¼ inch from folded edges, stretching elastic as you sew to fit the doll's wrist.
Sew gathering line at top of sleeves. Ease fullness and stitch sleeves to bodice. Sew side seams of sleeves and bodice.
Fold neck ruffle strip in half lengthwise, with right sides facing. Sew short ends together *using ¼-inch seams*; turn to right side. Sew a gathering thread ¼ inch from raw edge and gather to fit neck edge.
Turn back ⅛ inch the facing on bodice center back. With right sides facing, sew ruffle to neck edge (sew ruffle on back bodice just to center back). Fold the back bodice facing over the ruffle ends, right sides facing, and stitch in place. Trim seam and turn facing right side out.
Topstitch the ruffle seam allowance close to neck seam line.
Using ½-inch seams, sew short side of skirt together, leaving a 2½-inch opening at top (center back); press seam open. Stitch gathering threads along top edge; gather to fit bodice and pin in place. Fold bodice back facings over gathers, right sides facing, and sew in place; turn to right side and press.
Press under raw edge at bottom of skirt for a finished length of 7½ inches; hem. Sew snaps to bodice.

APRON: For the bib, cut two 2¾x3-inch pieces from muslin and a matching piece from fleece. Sandwich fleece between muslin pieces and zigzag-stitch around edges. Thread ribbon in eyelets of lace trim. Sew lace across bib top. Cut two 8-inch pieces of lace and sew to bib sides. Begin sewing edges of lace at sides of bib at waist, leaving unstitched lace free for straps.

Appliqué a small heart (pattern 1 on page 72) to the bib front, positioning it ½ inch from the waistline edge. Machine-quilt around heart.

For the skirt, cut a 7x17-inch rectangle from muslin. With right sides facing, sew bias plaid strip to bottom of skirt ¾ inch from bottom edge, using ¼-inch seam. Press seam downward. Sew lace, with threaded ribbon, atop bottom of bias strip, covering raw edges of strip. Machine-hem the short sides.

Run a gathering stitch along the top edge of skirt ¼ inch from edge and gather to 6 inches. Center bib to center of gathered skirt and sew together, right sides facing, using ¼ inch seam.

Cut a 1¼x6½-inch strip from muslin for waistband. Press under ¼ inch on long edges. Cut two 2x16-inch strips from muslin for apron ties; hem on long sides and one short side. Sew raw ends of ties to ends of waistband. Encase raw edges of gathered skirt and bib with waistband.

Press bib upward. Sew straps to back of waistband.

Brush cheeks of doll with powdered rouge.

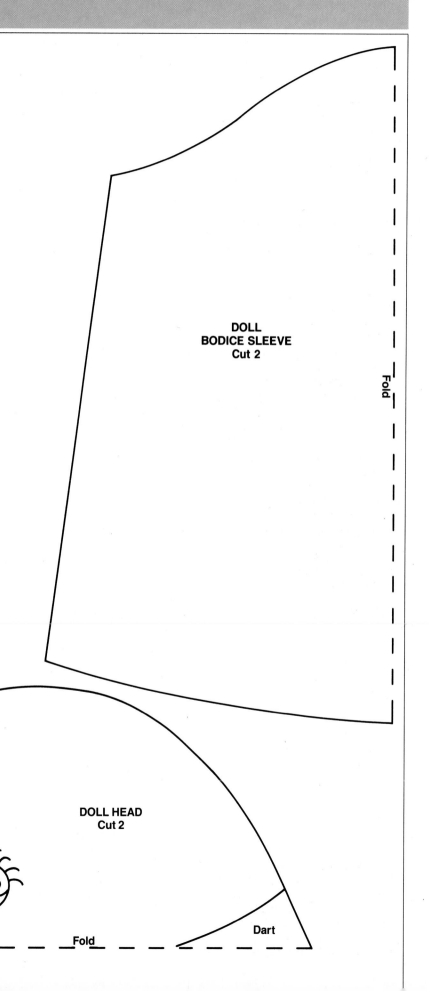

DOLL
BODICE SLEEVE
Cut 2

Fold

DOLL HEAD
Cut 2

Open

Fold

Dart

HEARTFELT DESIGNS

Holiday Rag Doll

Full size patterns *(continued)*

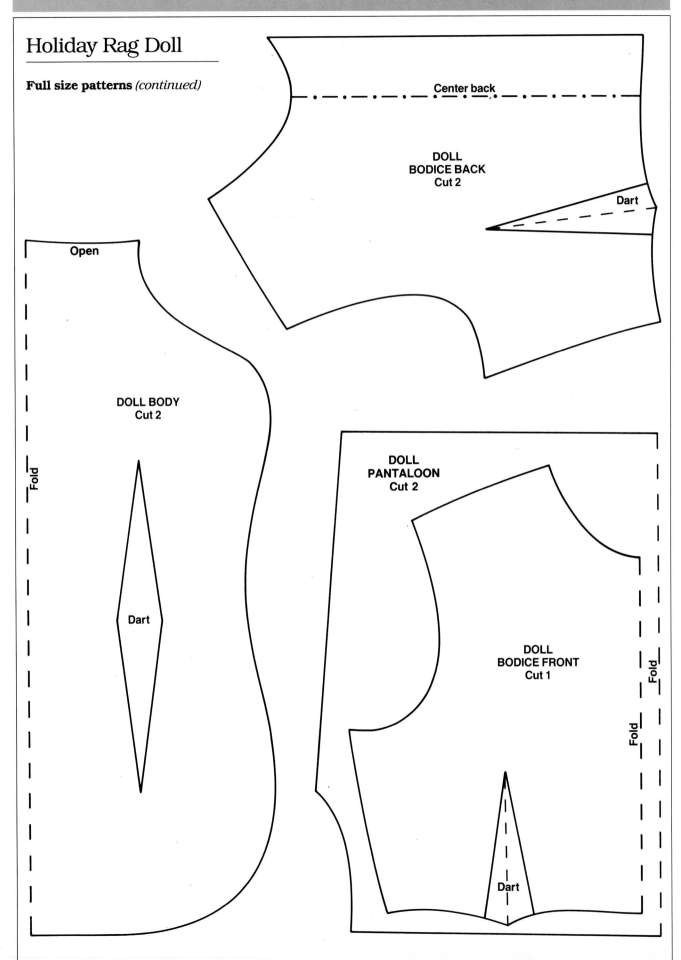

Center back

DOLL
BODICE BACK
Cut 2

Dart

Open

DOLL BODY
Cut 2

Fold

Dart

DOLL
PANTALOON
Cut 2

DOLL
BODICE FRONT
Cut 1

Fold

Fold

Fold

Dart

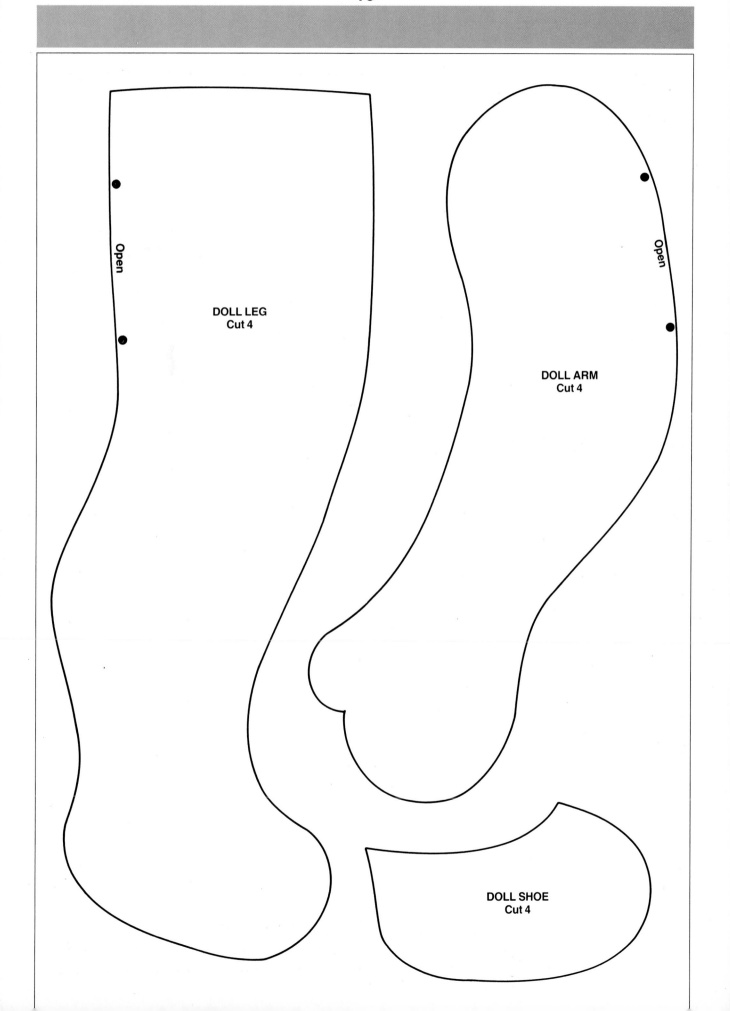

DOLL LEG
Cut 4

Open

DOLL ARM
Cut 4

Open

DOLL SHOE
Cut 4

ACKNOWLEDGMENTS

Our special thanks to the following designers, who contributed projects to this book. When more than one project appears on a page, the acknowledgment specifically cites the project with the page number. A page number alone indicates one designer contributed all of the projects listed on that page.

Donna Barnett-Albert—4–5; 13; 14–15

Taresia Boernke—6–7; 38–39; 40–41

Lenda DuBose—12

Phyllis Dunstan—8–9, bear sewing caddy; 44, toy airplane

Claudia Pesek—10–11

Margaret Sindelar—8–9, album cover; 66–67; 68–69; 70–71

Sara Jane Treinen—8–9, peg rack; 42–43, shutters, pillow sham; 45, bulletin board and pillows

A special thank-you to the following people, who loaned us quilts that were used as projects:

Doris Groff-Garland—32–33; 58–59

Glin Heisey—42–43

For their cooperation and courtesy, we extend a special thanks to the following sources:

DMC Corporation (for floss used on photo album on page 8)
   197 Trumbull Street
   Elizabeth, NJ 07206

J.P. Stevens (for Laura Ashley bed linens on pages 40–41)
   1185 Avenue of the Americas
   New York, NY 10036

Laura Ashley (for wallpapers and lampshade on pages 42–45)
   714 Madison Avenue
   New York, NY 10021

paper white, ltd. (for linens on pages 30–31)
   P.O. Box 956
   Fairfax, CA 94930

Plain n' Fancy (for piano bench on page 13)
   P.O. Box 357
   Mathews, VA 23109

A special thank-you to the following people, whose technical skills are greatly appreciated.

Pam Bono

Christopher Cravens

Kathy Engel

Susan Knight

Patty Ptasnik

Mary Shaddy

Margaret Sindelar

Judith Veeder

Don Wipperman

Chris Neubauer

We also are pleased to acknowledge the following photographers, whose talents and technical skills contributed much to this book.

Hopkins Associates—4–5; 6–7; 8–9; 10–11; 12–13; 38–39; 40–41; 42–43; 44–45; 60; 66–67; 68–69; 70

Mike Jensen—14–15; 30–31; 32–33; 58–59; 61

Perry Struse—71